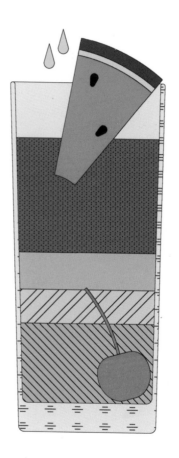

TEQUILA

Shake, Muddle, Stir

Tequila: Shake, Muddle, Stir by Dan Jones

First published in 2018 by Hardie Grant Books,
an imprint of Hardie Grant Publishing

Hardie Grant Books (UK)
52–54 Southwark Street
London SE1 1UN

Hardie Grant Books (Australia)
Ground Floor, Building 1
658 Church Street
Melbourne, VIC 3121

hardiegrantbooks.com

British Library Cataloguing-in-Publication Data. A catalogue record
for this book is available from the British Library.

ISBN: 978-1-78488-165-8

Publisher: Kate Pollard
Publishing Assistant: Eila Purvis
Art Direction: Matt Phare
Illustrator: Daniel Servansky
Recipe development: Seb Munsch
Copy editor: Kay Delves
Proofreader: Andrea O'Connor
Indexer: Cathy Heath
Colour Reproduction by p2d

Printed and bound in China by Leo Paper Group

TEQUILA

Shake, Muddle, Stir

by Dan Jones

ILLUSTRATIONS BY DANIEL SERVANSKY

hardie grant books

CONTENTS

Welcome to

to

TEQUILA

Shake, Muddle, Stir

'First you take a drink, then the drink takes a drink, then the drink takes you.' – F. Scott Fitzgerald

It's 3 a.m. You're about to pull a French exit, but a devilish friend with a Cheshire-cat grin waddles onto the dance floor balancing a sticky bar tray studded with tequila in plastic shot glasses, withered lemon slices and a ketchup-crusted salt shaker. You shudder it down; your mouth caves in and the warmth engulfs you. Suddenly, it's noon the following day and – in between popping painkillers and sipping 18 cups of black coffee – tiny memory bombs are going off in your head: lasers and Ke$ha remixes, borrowing someone's glitter lip balm in the bathrooms, inappropriate nudity, signing up for a 7 a.m. Booty Blast class and bulk-buying charcoal face masks online. Oh, and there's chilli sauce on your sheets.

There's nothing wrong with crossing your fingers and chugging it back, but there are myriad marvellous ways to enjoy Mexico's premier spirit. The finest tequila can embody hundreds of different flavours and aromas, from citrus, mint and verdant green leaves, to almond, oak and honey, to butterscotch, vanilla and leather, while mezcal – tequila's errant cousin – has its own smoky, earthy and downright dirty and delightful palate. Sip slowly over crushed ice or enjoy in the world's tastiest, eye-crossing cocktails.

This is *Tequila: Shake, Muddle, Stir*. How to mix it, shake it, stir it and – most importantly – how to drink it. A full list of mix-at-home recipes, infusions and syrups, with essential and impressive tools, glassware, marvellous mixers, butt-tingling bitters and the world's very best tequilas – from Mexican classics to smoky, fresh and young indie upstarts from the wrong side of the tracks.

Now, let's slam it back.

Dan Jones

WORTH A SHOT: THE STORY OF TEQUILA

Guadalajaran skies, desert heat, verdant blue-green leaves, distilled down via an ancient recipe into a crystal-clear, power-punch of a spirit. The roots of our most beloved, hangover-inducing inebriant go all the way back to the 13th century. Agave was an important part of life in pre-Hispanic Mexico: the dense fibres were perfect for mats, ropes, possibly wigs, but people also had another use for the plant: they loved to booze around with agave juice. *Pulque* was their favourite drink, a fermented, milky coloured, yeasty agave juice concoction

that pre-Aztec civilisations had the good sense to distil.

North American fascination with tequila began during prohibition, and surfaced again in World War II when European spirits were hard to come by. However, it wasn't until 1944 that the Mexican government decreed the spirit could only be made in Jalisco, Mexico. There have been tweaks and upgrades to the laws of tequila production ever since but, like Champagne and cognac, it remains a product of origin and can only legally be made in the states of Jalisco, Tamaulipas, Nayarit, Michoacán and Guanajuato. Today, there are more than 100 distilleries in Mexico that proudly create over 900 brands of tequila (and more than 2,000 new brand names have been registered), much to the delight of Margarita-lovers, spirit-sippers and side-boob-showing LA wellness Instagrammers (it's only 64 kcal a shot. #blessed).

TEQUILA: THE SCIENCE BIT

The recipe for tequila is startlingly simple. All you need is agave, yeast and water, a few years for your crops to mature, oh, and a donkey or two.

Jimadores (agave farmers) harvest the *piña* (heart) from the centre of the huge Weber blue agave at the perfect point in its life cycle (by all accounts, a rare, almost esoteric skill passed down through generations). The piña is chopped up and gently steam-baked in a brick oven for a few days (or in an industrial pressure cooker for a shorter cook time) and – slowly – the heart softens as the starch turns to sugar. The cooked piña is shredded like pulled pork, then crushed (often on a stone wheel, sometimes by donkeys) to extract the *aguamiel*, or juice, which is poured into heated wooden tanks.

The nectar ferments for a week or two – the yeast found naturally on the leaves of the agave plant is traditionally used to speed up the process – and then it's distilled two to three times, water is added and it's aged in wooden tanks or vats. Each producer's distillation process, aging time and vessel give the tequila its unique flavour notes and aroma. It takes between 14 and 21 days to create the perfect white, clear-as-crystal tequila, while aging the spirit for two months creates a pale gold tequila, drawing in some of the flavours and hues of the wood. Aging the spirit from two to 364 days creates *reposado* (rested) tequila, and one year and beyond is known as *anejo* or aged tequila (and it's delicious).

As a product of origin, tequila can only be created in five Mexican municipalities, but almost every drop of tequila you

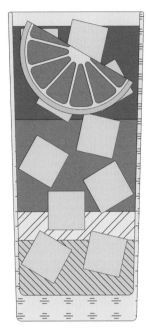

The production of mezcal is similar to tequila, though a little less regulated, meaning it is produced in eight Mexican states. If tequila is the fruit of a gently caressed, steam-bathed process, mezcal is a made with a little more thrill: piña from agave (not usually Weber blue) is roasted in underground pits, giving it its trademark smoky, earthy tang.

There's a twist in the story of tequila and mezcal, and it's to do with the agave plant. There are roughly 200 types of agave, most are native to Mexico, and only 40 are made into liquor. To reach premium ripeness, the plant has a slow – sometimes decades-long – maturation. This makes it difficult to farm, and even harder to anticipate just how much you'll need in, say, 15 years time. Add to that the fact that to harvest agave is to kill the plant itself and it means many are worried about it becoming endangered.

drink is made in the Mexican state of Jalisco. Premium tequila makers pride themselves on using '100 per cent blue agave,' although the legal requirement is only 51 per cent. Tequila is sometimes blended with a neutral spirit made from cane sugar, creating a mixto tequila, which is almost always of a lower quality.

The World's Best Tequilas and Mezcals

TRIED AND TESTED, MIXED AND SIPPED, SPILT AND MOPPED UP: THESE ARE THE WORLD'S VERY BEST TEQUILAS AND MEZCALS, FROM RELIABLE OLD-TIMERS TO YOUNG UPSTARTS.

BEST FOR: MARGARITAS

PATRÓN SILVER TEQUILA

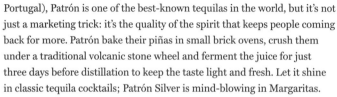

A powerful, bright and sunshine-smooth sipper. From Mexico's Jalisco region, Patrón is the industry giant that still crafts its tequila by hand, and the brand's Patrón Silver is world class. Known for its squat, semi-recycled bottles and bulbous corks (imported from near Lisbon, Portugal), Patrón is one of the best-known tequilas in the world, but it's not just a marketing trick: it's the quality of the spirit that keeps people coming back for more. Patrón bake their piñas in small brick ovens, crush them under a traditional volcanic stone wheel and ferment the juice for just three days before distillation to keep the taste light and fresh. Let it shine in classic tequila cocktails; Patrón Silver is mind-blowing in Margaritas.

BEST FOR: CELEB SIPPERS

CASAMIGOS AÑEJO TEQUILA

With smouldering silver fox George Clooney as co-founder, Casamigos has something of an unfair advantage: the tequila house has inherited more than a little Hollywood glamour. Thank goodness, then, that Casamigos Añejo lives up to the hype. It's pants-down delicious. Aged for 14 months in white oak barrels, this highland tequila is a spicy little number with a soft vanilla tone and fresh mint finish. Casamigos' blanco and reposado are fine spirits, too: the former is verdant, vegetal and bright.

BEST FOR: TRADITIONALISTS

QUIQUIRIQUI MEZCAL

Handcrafted in Mexico, Quiquiriqui is a small-batch brand of single-estate mezcals that boasts zero industrial jiggery pokery in favour of age-old growing, harvesting, squishing and roasting techniques. Espadin agave juice is fermented in oak vats using airborne yeast, then double distilled in small pot stills to create Quiquiriqui's rounded, peppery Matatlan Mezcal. Their San Juan Del Rio is made by a fourth-gen producer and has a zingy, zippy citrus tone with a smoky, peppery bite. And Quiquiriqui Tobala uses a rare, high altitude, wild agave that's pit-roasted and has a buttery popcorn edge. It's usually a single-batch release, so sip it while you can.

BEST FOR: MYTH-LOVERS

MEZCAL EL SILENCIO

El Silencio trades on the myths of Mexico's Oaxaca region, the true heartland of mezcal. The brand's enigmatic edge is inspired by its complex, full-blooded flavour structure. El Silencio Espadin has subtle notes of roasted sweet and sticky fig, charred fruit stones and a soft, spicy aroma stored in the dark in a black clay and obsidian bottle. El Silencio Joven Ensamble is a premium organic agave mezcal, blended to create a super-smooth drop with all the fruit, spice and smoke you'd expect, but with a tickle of fennel, jasmine and white pepper. It's a dramatic sipping mezcal, and it's perfect for sipping too.

BEST FOR:
UPSCALE DRINKERS

GRAN CENTENARIO
REPOSADO TEQUILA

Rested for six months in French oak barrels, the angel-powered Gran Centenario Reposado has a buttery, golden tone. Created with highland Weber blue agave, this much-loved, ultra-premium tequila is considered the perfect reposado. Founded by one-time Mexican tavern owner Lazaro Gallardo in the late 1800s (and first bottled in the 1920s), it's a super-smooth yet peppery drop with cinnamon, pineapple and caramel notes. Perfect for sipping over ice, the art deco-style bottle (featuring an agave-obsessed angel) will look eye-catching on any vintage drinks trolley or spin the bottle contest.

BEST FOR:
TEQUILA GEEKS

TAPATIO BLANCO TEQUILA

Tapatio tequila gives the bar trade fizzy knickers; it's the cult brand that has a smooth, premium taste at an old-school price. The blanco is handcrafted in the highlands of Jalisco, Mexico, using agave from Carlos Camarena's estate and settles in steel tanks for just one month after a double distillation that takes the spirit to its final proof (rather than blending it back down to a sippable strength with spring water). Tapatio blanco has a delightfully bright, juicy and spicy flavour with notes of roasted agave, desert herbs and a little licorice for good measure. A great starter-tequila for the home-cocktail maker.

BEST FOR:
SMOOTH SIPPERS

TEQUILA OCHO

Tequila super-fan and restaurateur Tomas Estes loves
the spirit so much he decided to make his own. In
collaboration with hallowed producers, the Camarena
estate (of Tapatio tequila fame), Tequila Ocho is
unique in its approach: it celebrates the vintage of
each batch, underlining its date and terroir, and
highlighting the subtle differences between each
harvest. While most tequilas are distilled for a
consistent flavour, Ocho allows the ingredients
to speak for themselves. Each bottle is a delicious
and criminally smooth sipper.

BEST FOR:
CITRUS LOVERS

OLMECA ALTOS PLATA TEQUILA

This delightful, award-winning little brand
uses plump, fruity agave from the highlands
of Los Altos to create its plata-style tequila:
a herby, citrussy drop that's subtle and sweet.
It's created by one-time bartenders Henry
Besant and Dre Masso (with Maestro
Tequilero Jesús Hernández) who wanted
a sipping spirit that also shone out in
cocktails. Olmeca Altos is a labour of love,
and it shows: it's a fan favourite.

BEST FOR:
SHOWING OFF

CASA DRAGONES TEQUILA

Female tequila-makers are few and far between; Maestra Tequilera and co-owner Bertha González Nieves launched her Casa Dragones brand in 2009, and it soon found its way to the top of the list of premium, upscale (and eye-wateringly expensive) spirits. Casa Dragones is something rather special. It's a joven tequila, a blend of blanco and extra añejo, that's filtered to a super-pale 'platinum' tone and comes with a fanfare of agave to orange blossom, hazelnut and pear. It's known for its modern, crafty take on the age-old spirit: volcanic soil, small-batch distillation, hand-signed bottles. Best served as a sipper (Bertha recommends the Riedel Ouverture glass to get the full aroma).

BEST FOR:
TOUGH NUTS

EL LUCHADOR TEQUILA

Ready for the taste-equivalent of a pile-driver, Mexican masked wrestling's most spine-jolting move? Open your heart and mind to El Luchador, the 110-proof organic highland tequila that zings with lemon pepper, juicy agave and sea salt. Skipping the blending-with-water stage, this tequila is unaged and straight from the still, so it's powerful and bright-tasting, but surprisingly smooth and complex. The faint-hearted will want to sip El Luchador over ice to counteract the (albeit soft) burn.

Essential Tequila Gadgetry

**BUILD UP YOUR HOME BAR WITH A FEW
MINIMAL ESSENTIALS TO CREATE THE WORLD'S
MOST MARVELLOUS MARGARITAS, SIPPING
DRINKS AND PUNCHES.**

IMPRESSIVE TOOLS

Create your own at-home tequila bar with a range of nifty cocktail-making tools. Start off simple: a shaker, jigger, strainer and an ice bucket. Here's what you'll need to keep it minimal:

JIGGER

A toolbox essential. The jigger is the standard measure for spirits and liqueurs, and is available in many different sizes. Heavy metallic jiggers look the part, but plastic or glass versions also do the job. If you don't have a jigger or single-shot glass, use an egg cup as a stand-in – at least then your ratios will be right, even if your shots might be a little generous – failing that, cross your fingers and free-pour your drinks.

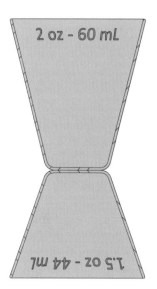

2 oz – 60 mL

1.5 oz – 44 mL

SAUCER

Some bartenders use a 'rimming dish' to add the salt or sugar rim to a glass but if you think, like me, that just sounds weird, then use a saucer with a larger diameter than the glass.

MIXING GLASS

A simple, sturdy straight-sided glass (also known as the Boston) – or a straight-sided pint glass that tapers out – for cocktails that need stirring with a bar spoon rather than shaking, or to allow for extra volume when attached to the can of your shaker (to make two or more drinks at a time).

The two halves are locked together and you shake until the drink is chilled, then a Hawthorne strainer (see opposite) can be used to strain the drink into a glass.

SHAKER

Sometimes known as the Boston shaker, it's the home mixer's silver bullet. This is your single most important piece of kit as very few cocktails are possible without one. The classic metallic model has three main parts: a base, known as the 'can' (a tall, tumbler shape that tapers out), a tight-fitting funnel top with built-in strainer, onto which a small cap fits (which can also be used as a jigger). It's brilliantly straightforward and, like all fine tools, it pays to keep it scrupulously clean. If you can't get your hands on one, consider a large glass jar with a lid and waterproof seal.

HAWTHORNE STRAINER

This showy-looking strainer, trimmed with a spring, comes in handy when your shaker's built-in version isn't up to the job. Place on a glass and pour the cocktail through it, or hold up against the cocktail can or mixing glass and pour from a height. Wash immediately after use. A fine tea strainer does the job brilliantly, but the classic Hawthorne really looks the part.

BLENDER

Essential for fruity little numbers. Unless you're using a NutriBullet, most domestic blenders find ice a challenge, so it's best to use crushed ice in blended cocktails. Add your ingredients first, then the ice, and start off on a slow speed before turning it up to max. No need to strain. Once the consistency is super smooth, pour into a glass and serve.

CHOPPING BOARD AND KNIFE

Simple, but essential. Keep the board clean, the knife super sharp and practise your peeling skills: the aim is to avoid as much white pith as possible, leaving just the peel that is studded with aromatic oils.

ICE BUCKET

The centrepiece of your home bar. It can be simple, functional and slightly retro, or the full plastic pineapple. An insulated ice bucket means your ice cubes will keep their shape for longer, and a good set of vintage tongs adds a touch of class.

UPSCALE EXTRAS

ICE PICK

Buy bags of filtered crushed ice or cubes (and always buy double or triple the amount you think you'll need), or attack your own homemade ice block with an ice pick. Boil water, let it cool slightly and pour into an old plastic ice-cream container. Freeze solid, turn out onto a clean tea (dish) towel, and then attack as needed with a firm grip. The ice will go everywhere, but bear with it. Keep the shards large and jagged.

MUDDLER

A short, usually wooden baton used to mash and muddle fruit, herbs, ice and sugar in the glass, bruising and bashing up the ingredients to release their natural oils and flavours. Think of it as a pestle for your drink. If you don't have a muddler, use a flat-ended rolling pin.

NOVELTY STRAWS, PARASOLS AND PLASTIC MONKEYS

Tricky. Creating hands-down amazing cocktails means that they should taste and look otherworldly just as they are. That's without parasols, plastic monkeys, flashing LED ice cubes and novelty straws you can also wear as glasses. That said, there's something more than a little pleasing about adding the odd frill to your drink. Make sure paper straws are part of your home bar toolkit – stripy red and white ones are pretty eye-catching – and the odd plastic monkey never hurt anyone. Maybe save your penis straws for extra-special occasions, like 80th birthday parties or funerals – things like that.

CITRUS PRESS

Always, always, always use fresher-than-fresh citrus juices. Never skimp on this part of drink-making. If you don't have a citrus press or squeezer, use your hands. Roll and squish your fruit on a hard surface to loosen it up, slice in half, then squeeze through your fingers, catching the pips as you go.

BAR SPOON

The classic bar spoon has a long, twisted (or sometimes flat) handle, a flat end and a teardrop-shaped spoon used for stirring and measuring out ingredients. It's not essential, but it looks pretty cool.

CANELE OR JULIENNE KNIFE

A fancy bit of kit: the canele knife has a V-shaped groove for cutting citrus peel spirals, carving melons and probably many other crafty uses. Not essential, but great to have.

COCKTAIL STICK

For spearing cherries, citrus peel, fruit slices, olives, onion slivers, pickles, sausages, cleaning under your nails, etc.

SWIZZLE STICK

More than just cocktail furniture, the swizzle allows the drinker to navigate their own drink, stirring as they go. Great for drinks packed with fruit or garnishes, or for nervous partygoers who need something to fiddle with.

A Guide to Glasses

YOU CAN SERVE A DELICIOUS TEQUILA COCKTAIL
IN JUST ABOUT ANYTHING: A CHIPPED COFFEE
MUG, DORA THE EXPLORER PARTY CUPS, A SHOE,
BUT IT'S BEST TO INVEST IN THE PROPER
GLASSWARE – AND KEEP EACH ONE
SQUEAKY CLEAN.

COUPE

The short, trumpet-shaped glass perfect for Champagne and sparkling wines and a respectable Martini glass alternative. Invest in a vintage set – it's worth it.

MARTINI

Cocktail culture's most iconic glass: the refined stem and cone-shaped glass flares out to create a large, shallow recess. Somehow loses its ability not to slosh out its contents as the evening wears on. (**Fig. 1**)

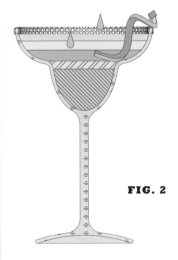

FIG. 2

MARGARITA

There's no other way to drink a Margie than from its official wide glass; it's the wonky, one-toothed cousin of the Martini glass with a bulbous bottom and a yearning to meet the lips of a handsome stranger. (**Fig. 2**)

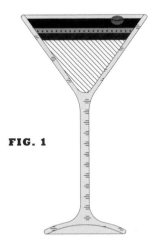

FIG. 1

JULEP CUP

The little, stainless steel or copper cup that frosts in seconds and fits neatly inside most shakers. A hangover from 1800s Kentucky cocktail culture.

SHOT GLASS

Short and simple. Pour, drink, slam down. Done. Also doubles as a jigger. (**Fig. 3**)

TUMBLER

The short glass that's perfect for short or single-shot drinks. Like most things, best to pick one with a heavy bottom. (**Fig. 4**)

HIGHBALL

Ostensibly a tall glass with a thick and sturdy bottom that holds 225–350 ml (8–12 oz) perfectly mixed booze. (**Fig. 5**)

LARGE WINE GLASS

The one your Auntie Sharon drinks her chardonnay from and then demands to speak to the manager. (**Fig. 6**)

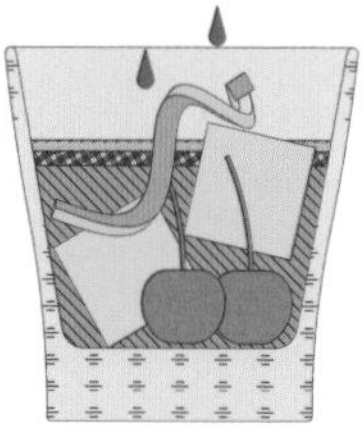

FIG. 5

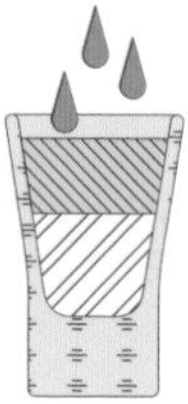

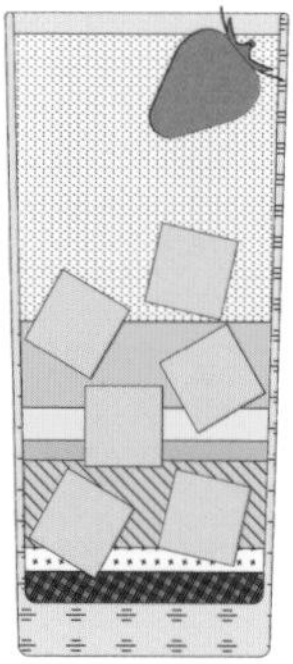

FIG. 6

FIG. 3

FIG. 4

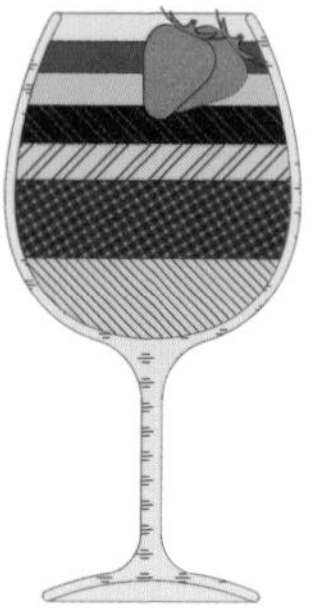

FIG. 7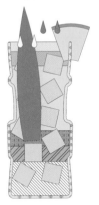

FIG. 8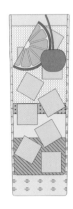

FIG. 9

TIKI GLASS

The tiki glass was born in mid-20th-century American tiki bars and attributed to Don the Beachcomber, the founding father of tiki culture. It's a tall, wonky-looking glass with a face like an Easter Island statue. (**Fig. 7**)

COLLINS GLASS

The skinny, usually straight-sided version of the highball. (**Fig. 8**)

JAM JAR

There are no hard-and-fast rules for how to serve your drinks – or rather what you serve them in. You can use any number of alternatives – jam jars, tea cups, sciencey test tubes and beakers, Russian tea glasses and shoes – to get your guests beyond the pale. (**Fig. 9**)

PUNCH GLASS

Ornate, sometimes with handles, and small-ish so your guests don't get too tipsy too quickly.

Tricks of the Trade

IT'S NOT JUST THE QUALITY OF YOUR TOOL, IT'S HOW YOU USE IT. HOW TO SHAKE, MUDDLE, STIR, AND MIX IT ALL UP.

HOW TO DO IT

HOW TO SHAKE

There's a war going on in cocktail land. How long to shake to get the perfect concoction? No one can agree. Some say 15 seconds of brisk shaking, others say less. This book is going out on a limb and settles on a short and sharp seven seconds. Any longer could dilute the drink a little too much, affecting potency. Otherwise, there should be no bottle-flipping or sparkler-lighting, although a little lemon-and-lime juggling wouldn't go amiss.

HOW TO STIR

Whip out your bar spoon and your mixing glass, and stir drinks gently and deftly with ice to chill the concoction. When condensation forms on the outside of the glass, it's ready to go.

HOW TO CHILL

If you have room, clear a shelf in your freezer and keep your cocktail glasses on ice, or pack them full of cubes to throw away when the glass is chilled.

POTENCY

All cocktails are potent, but some are more potent than others. Each drink should seek to achieve a perfect balance of flavours and can attempt differing levels of intensity, but shouldn't get you drunk – at least not on its own. Perfect measurements really matter.

THE LOOK

Fresh garnishes, squeaky clean glasses, clear, purified ice and a perfect balance of colours and visible textures are essential.

AROMATICS

Your drink should smell really, really great – not just taste good. Bitters, fresh juices and citrus peels packed with fragrant oils help achieve this.

TEQUILA, MEZCAL & MORE: HOW TO PUT YOUR BACK BAR TOGETHER

A few bottles of amazing tequila? Check. Smoky, hell-fumed mezcal? Check. But what about everything else? Create a back bar with a mix of strong, clean and classic spirits, the odd special buy, and a few rarities.

Depending on your budget, you don't necessarily need to stock up on fine vintage spirits for cocktail mixing – their subtler qualities are sometimes lost in the mixing – but you do need to invest in something of good, basic quality.

TEQUILAS & MEZCALS

More of the world's best agave-based brain melters later, but unaged (or aged for no more than 60 days in steel containers) silver (*blanco*) tequila is an essential part of your back bar. Tequila gold is sweet and smooth, coloured and flavoured with a note of caramel, *reposado* (rested) tequila, aged in wooden tanks or barrels, brings a deep, leathery undertone to your mixes.

BITTERS

Said to be a cure for hiccups, Angostura (the Venezuelan-by-way-of-Trinidad-and-Tobago) bitters are an essential element of the back bar. The part-herbal, part-alcoholic tincture is highly aromatic, giving cocktails a depth and complexity of taste, and colouring white spirits a subtle, sunrise pink. Bitters and cordial producers Fee Brothers (est. 1863) is another good brand

to start with: their whisky barrel-aged bitters, rhubarb and plum flavours are particularly mouth-caving.

SYRUP

Essential. Simple syrup – aka gomme or sugar syrup – is liquid sugar and, mixed part-for-part with sharp citrus juices, brings a delightfully sweet-sour note to a drink. Buy a premium version of simple syrup (Monin is a good, decent brand) or make your own (page 38).

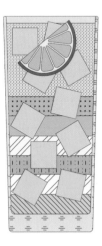

GIN

The little 'shot of lightening' has come a long way since its humble beginnings as the demonic hell broth of the London underworld. Handcrafted, premium gins have elevated this powerful spirit to otherworldly proportions.

CAMPARI AND APEROL

Sharp, ruby-red, smooth yet bitter spirits that pep up cocktails and form the basis of the Negroni and Americano. They are really quite life-changing mixed with soda water and chilled sparkling wine.

CASSIS

Invest in a good-quality crème de cassis or crème de mûre: dark berry-flavoured liqueurs for Kirs and Kir Royales, and more besides – they're the perfect sweetener in pared-down gin recipes. Mix a drop of cassis in a Gin and Tonic to give it a sweet berry kick.

VERMOUTH

The fortified wine packed with botanicals, in sweet or dry versions. Get both and keep them refrigerated after opening.

VODKA

Stolichnaya, Smirnoff and Absolut are all reliable brands, while the more expensive Crystal Head vodka – encased in a skull-shaped bottle – certainly looks the part.

WHISKY

For mixing, pick a sturdy, deep-tasting bourbon rather than an aged malt. Monkey Shoulder, Knob Creek and Bullet Bourbon are all strong contenders.

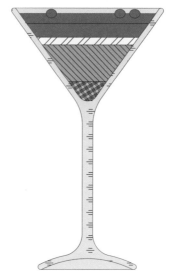

MIXERS

They say no one uses cola as a mixer any more. No one. (Although you're permitted a splash in a Long Island Iced Tea.) Make sure you have the odd can to hand, and keep ginger beer or ale in stock, as well as sparkling water, prosecco, cava or Champagne, and freshly squeezed citrus juices, coconut water and – always – a truckload of ice.

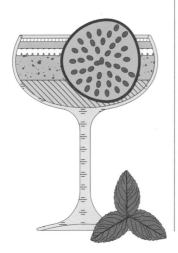

Infusions, Syrups and Flavoured Salts: How to Make Your Own

CREATE YOUR OWN DELICIOUS INFUSED SIPPING TEQUILA, THE PERFECT COCKTAIL SYRUPS AND FLAVOURED SALTS. FROM A CAFFEINE-PACKED COFFEE TEQUILA TO A SPICY CHILLI NUMBER THAT'LL MAKE STEAM BLOW OUT OF YOUR EARS.

INFUSIONS

COFFEE TEQUILA

Perfect for coffee geeks who love to booze: a vanilla-powered infusion that's simple to make and even easier to drink. Slip a shot of this in your travel mug.

INGREDIENTS

1 split vanilla pod (bean)
600 ml (20 oz) blanco tequila
100 g (3½ oz) freshly ground coffee
100 ml (3½ oz) Demerara Simple Syrup (page 38)

METHOD Add a vanilla pod to your tequila and leave to infuse for 24–72 hours (check daily as you want a gentle vanilla taste; if you leave it too long it becomes too floral). When your vanilla infusion is ready, remove the vanilla pod, then add the ground coffee and give it a good shake. Place the tequila in the freezer for at least 72 hours. Strain through a coffee filter, then add a little of the simple syrup, to taste. Shake well.

TIP Best served in an Espresso Martini or straight from the freezer over ice as a sipping drink.

CINNAMON TEQUILA

A spicy, subtly sweet cinnamon-infused tequila that's delicious in a spiked hot chocolate or sipped over ice.

INGREDIENTS

600 ml (20 oz) tequila
150 ml (5 oz) Simple Syrup (page 38)
3 cinnamon sticks
1 tbsp cinnamon extract

METHOD Pour the tequila, syrup and cinnamon sticks into a large container and leave to steep in the fridge for 24–72 hours. Strain and add the cinnamon extract.

TIP Great in hot chocolate, add a dash to coffee or simply serve ice cold as a sipping drink.

CHILLI TEQUILA

From a subtly spicy jalapeño to a mind-blowing scotch bonnet, a chilli infusion can be as mild or as nuclear-hot as you like. You can use any chilli variety, but the hotter the chilli, the less time is needed for it to infuse.

INGREDIENTS

3 hot chillies
1 bottle blanco tequila

METHOD Cut the chillies into quarters and place in the tequila bottle. Leave to infuse at room temperature for at least 24 hours, then check daily after that. Remove the chillies when you've reached your desired heat. Strain and rebottle.

TIP Great in a Bloody Maria or served as a shot. Use it in any tequila cocktail where you want some extra spice.

\\

SYRUPS

Ah, the sweet stuff. A dash of sugar syrup can turn the most aggressive, put-hair-on-your-chest spirit into soda-pop. And it's very nearly foolproof to make. Follow the recipe on page 38 to create a Simple or Demerara Syrup (using either plain or demerara sugar), bottle and keep in the fridge for up to six weeks. Create your own with a little added spice, from star anise to cinnamon, or keep it fruity with pomegranate or winter berries. Each syrup recipe below makes enough dashes for about 15 drinks.

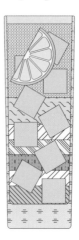

SWEET & SOUR MIX

Sweet & Sour is the name given to the perfect balance of sugar syrup and fresh citrus juice that can be made ahead of time (it's equal parts simple syrup and citrus juice) or created in small amounts per drink.

SIMPLE SYRUP

INGREDIENTS

200 ml (7 oz) water
100 g (3½ oz) demerara, cane
or granulated (raw) sugar
1 tbsp golden syrup or corn
syrup (optional)

EQUIPMENT Non-stick
saucepan, wooden spoon,
funnel

GLASS 200 ml (7 oz)
sterilised kilner (mason) jar
or glass bottle with stopper

METHOD Boil the water in
the saucepan and gently add
the sugar. Turn down the heat
and stir constantly with a
wooden spoon for 3–5 minutes,
until all the sugar is dissolved,
and the syrup is clear. Turn off
the heat and leave to cool.
While still runny, pour into a
sterilised kilner jar or pour
through a funnel into a
sterilised glass bottle with
stopper. Adding a spoonful of golden syrup to the cooled mixture
will help keep it smooth. Store in the fridge for up to six weeks.

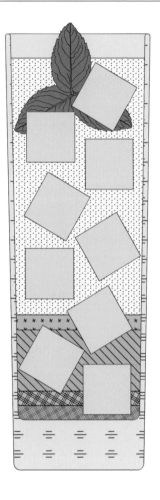

FLAVOURED SALTS

Create flavoured salt mixes to line the edge of your Margie and Bloody Maria glasses. Rimming jokes, notwithstanding.

CHILLI SALT

1 part chilli powder to 3 parts salt

LIME SALT

1 part zest of lime to 2 parts salt

TIP Leave the citrus to dry out a bit on a paper towel before adding to the salt.

BACON SALT

INGREDIENTS

500 g (1 lb 2 oz) smoked streaky bacon
1½ tbsp sea salt
2 tsp cracked black pepper

METHOD Preheat the oven to 180°C (350°F/Gas 4) and roast the bacon for 20–25 minutes until crispy. Allow to cool slightly, then chop the bacon finely by hand or in a food processor. Mix the bacon, salt and pepper together. Store in an airtight container for up to four weeks.

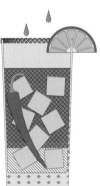

The Recipes

YOUR INGREDIENTS ARE ALL LINED UP, YOUR
CITRUS FRUITS ARE FRESH AND JUICY, AND YOUR
SHAKER, JIGGER AND GLASSWARE ARE ALL
SCRUPULOUSLY CLEAN. YOU'RE ALL SET.
NOW, ADD TEQUILA.

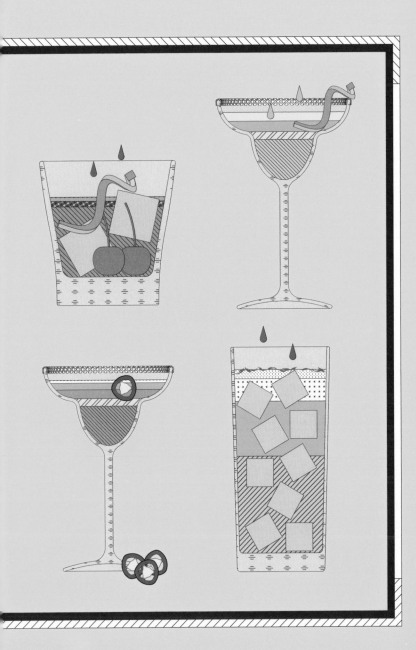

THE CLASSICS

AGE-OLD, CLASSIC TEQUILA CONCOCTIONS TOP
EVERY UPSCALE COCKTAIL LIST, AND SO THEY
SHOULD. PERFECTLY BALANCED, THESE
TEQUILA-POWERED RECIPES HIT THE SPOT
IN THE CLASSIEST WAY IMAGINABLE.

BLOODY MARIA

For those who like their Bloody Mary hot and spicy, this tequila-powered recipe uses Sangrita (an age-old, chilli-infused tomato juice and grenadine concoction) as its mixer, adding a complexity of flavours and aromas – and more than a little heat.

INGREDIENTS

1	lime wedge	for salt rim
2	Bacon Salt (page 39)	for salt rim
3	silver tequila	45 ml (1½ oz)
4	Sangrita Chaser (page 124)	120 ml (4 oz)
5	large green chilli	to garnish
6	hot sauce (optional)	dash

EQUIPMENT Bar spoon

METHOD Squish a lime wedge along the edge of a glass dip in the bacon salt. Fill the glass with ice and add the tequila and Sangrita Chaser. Stir carefully and garnish with a green chilli. Add a dash of hot sauce if you want extra spice.

GLASS TYPE:
HIGHBALL

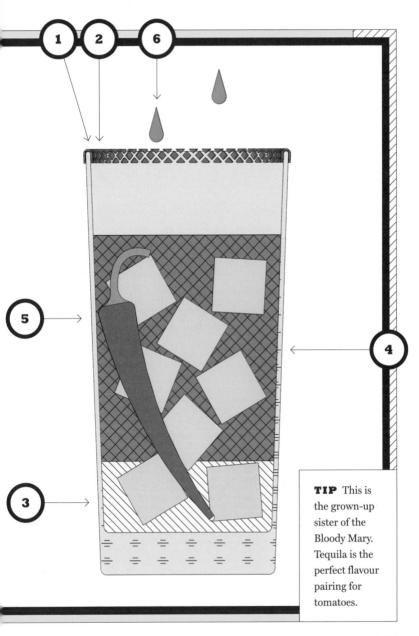

TIP This is the grown-up sister of the Bloody Mary. Tequila is the perfect flavour pairing for tomatoes.

TEQUILA SUNRISE

One sip of a Tequila Sunrise, with its novelty colour gradient from orange to blood-red and cherry, is like time travelling back to the 1980s. Drink with big hair, frosted eye shadow and the soundtrack to *Cocktail* on repeat.

INGREDIENTS

1	gold tequila	45 ml (1½ oz)
2	orange juice, freshly squeezed	90 ml (3 oz)
3	grenadine	dash
4	orange slice	to garnish
5	speared maraschino cherry	to garnish

EQUIPMENT Bar spoon

METHOD Fill a glass with ice, pour over the tequila and orange juice and stir gently with a bar spoon. Gently drop the grenadine onto the top so that it sinks down through the drink.
Garnish with a slice of orange and a speared cherry.

GLASS TYPE:
COLLINS

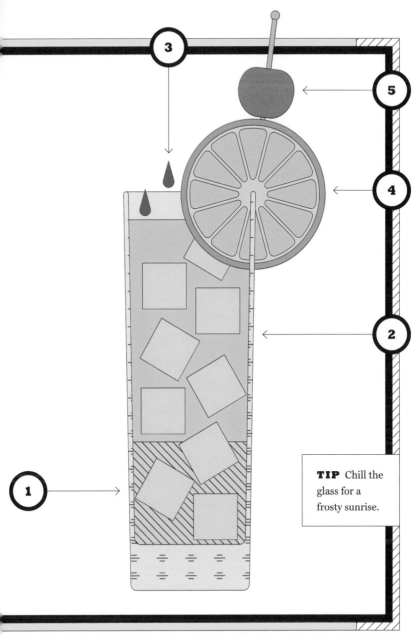

TIP Chill the glass for a frosty sunrise.

BEVERLY HILLS ICED TEA

A luxury version of the classic Long Island Iced Tea, swapping the quaint fishing villages of the New York State coastline for the sunshine glamour of Beverly Hills. This version is powered by buttery gold tequila and topped with Champagne.

INGREDIENTS

1	gold tequila	15 ml (½ oz)
2	vodka	15 ml (½ oz)
3	gold rum	15 ml (½ oz)
4	gin	15 ml (½ oz)
5	triple sec	15 ml (½ oz)
6	Sweet and Sour Mix (page 37)	30 ml (1 oz)
7	chilled Champagne	to top up
8	lemon wedge	to garnish

EQUIPMENT Shaker, strainer

METHOD Pour all of the ingredients (except the Champagne and lemon wedge) into a shaker filled with ice. Shake until cold and frothy, then strain into a chilled glass filled with ice. Top up with Champagne and drop a lemon wedge into the glass.

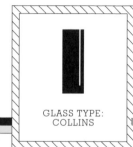

GLASS TYPE:
COLLINS

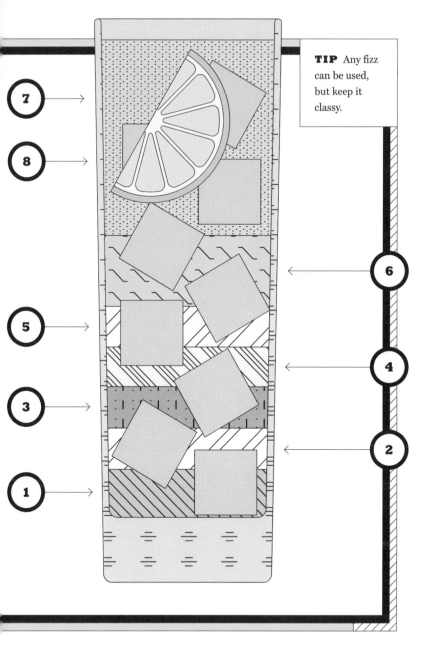

TEQUILA MOCKINGBIRD

This mint-edged, Kermit-coloured classic tequila cocktail is perfectly balanced with fresh lime. It's slightly more sour than sweet, and the reposado adds a rich, maple note.

INGREDIENTS

1	reposado tequila	60 ml (2 oz)
2	crème de menthe	15 ml (½ oz)
3	lime juice, freshly squeezed	15 ml (½ oz)
4	Simple Syrup (page 38)	7½ ml (¼ oz)
5	fresh mint leaf	to garnish

EQUIPMENT Shaker, strainer

METHOD Add all of the ingredients (except the garnish) to a shaker filled with ice. Shake vigorously until cold and strain into a chilled glass. Garnish with a mint leaf.

GLASS TYPE:
COUPE

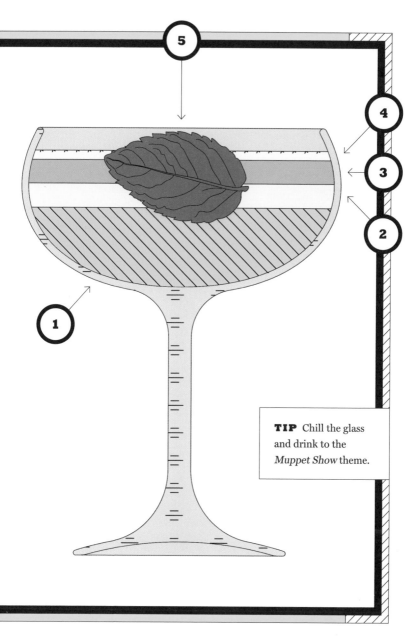

TIP Chill the glass and drink to the *Muppet Show* theme.

TEQRONI

Replacing gin with mezcal in the classic Negroni cocktail is a no-brainer; they both work perfectly with Campari or Aperol. Using reposado adds a subtle depth.

INGREDIENTS

1	mezcal	30 ml (1 oz)
2	Campari or Aperol	30 ml (1 oz)
3	sweet vermouth	30 ml (1 oz)
4	large orange twist	to garnish

EQUIPMENT Bar spoon

METHOD Combine the ingredients in an ice-filled glass. Stir for 15–20 seconds with a long bar spoon. Garnish with an orange twist.

GLASS TYPE:
TUMBLER

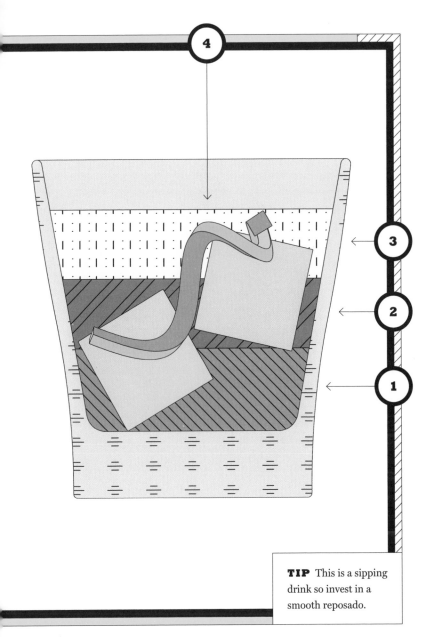

TIP This is a sipping drink so invest in a smooth reposado.

PALOMA

A fresh, zingy, almost-like-not-drinking-at-all way of drinking tequila.
This long cocktail, topped with chilled soda water uses reposado as its
base, pepped up with ruby grapefruit and lime juice. It's 100 per cent
refreshing: no wonder it's Mexico's favourite tequila cocktail.

INGREDIENTS

1	reposado tequila	60 ml (2 oz)
2	ruby grapefruit juice, freshly squeezed	½
3	lime juice, freshly squeezed	15 ml (½ oz)
4	agave syrup (or Simple Syrup, page 38)	15 ml (½ oz)
5	soda water	to top up
6	lime wheel	to garnish

EQUIPMENT Shaker, strainer

METHOD Pour the tequila, juices and syrup into an ice-filled shaker.
Shake vigorously and strain into an ice-filled glass. Top up with soda and
garnish with a lime wheel.

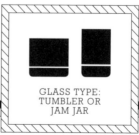

GLASS TYPE:
TUMBLER OR
JAM JAR

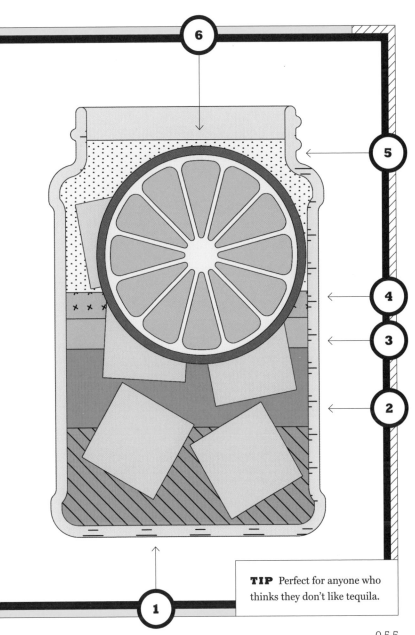

TIP Perfect for anyone who thinks they don't like tequila.

CHIMAYÓ

This classic autumnal cocktail, created by chef Arturo Jaramillo in the 60s, was inspired by the small, sweet, red chimayó apples of New Mexico. It's a simple recipe – deliciously sweet – and packs a kick.

INGREDIENTS

1	gold tequila	45 ml (1½ oz)
2	lemon juice, freshly squeezed	15 ml (½ oz)
3	crème de cassis	7½ ml (¼ oz)
4	cloudy apple juice	90 ml (3 oz)
5	apple slice	to garnish

EQUIPMENT Bar spoon

METHOD Pour all of the ingredients (except for the garnish) into a glass half-filled with ice, stir and garnish with the apple slice.

GLASS TYPE:
HIGHBALL

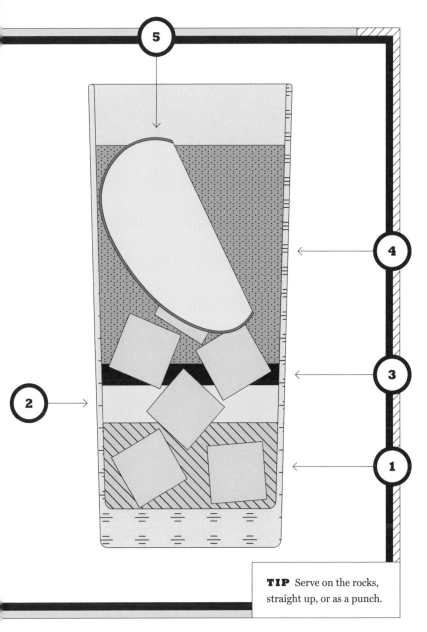

TIP Serve on the rocks, straight up, or as a punch.

JUAN COLLINS

Power-up a Tom Collins (created in the late 1870s by US cocktail legend, Jerry Thomas) with tequila rather than the classic gin. It's a pared down cocktail designed to reveal the quality of the tequila – so use a classy one.

INGREDIENTS

1	reposado tequila	45 ml (1½ oz)
2	lemon juice, freshly squeezed	30 ml (1 oz)
3	agave syrup	15 ml (½ oz)
4	soda water	60 ml (2 oz)
5	lime wedge	to garnish
6	maraschino cherry	to garnish

EQUIPMENT Bar spoon

METHOD Pour the tequila, lemon juice and agave syrup into a glass filled with ice. Stir and top up with soda. Squeeze the lime wedge over the drink and drop into the glass with a maraschino cherry.

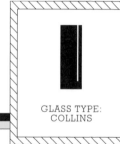

GLASS TYPE:
COLLINS

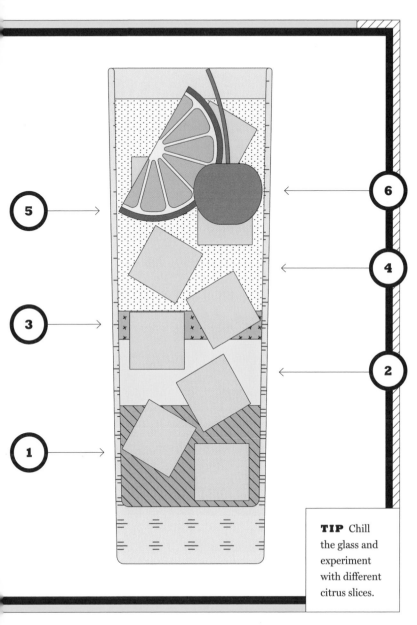

TIP Chill the glass and experiment with different citrus slices.

TEQUILA OLD FASHIONED

This version of the classic Old Fashioned swaps out whisky for a premium aged mezcal and the bitters give the drink a pale gold colour. Make sure the mezcal is extra fragrant and your orange twist is fresh, pungent and large enough to whack the drinker in the nose (it smells amazing).

INGREDIENTS

1	orange slice	1
2	cocktail cherries	2
3	mezcal	90 ml (3 oz)
4	agave syrup	7½ ml (¼ oz)
5	bitters	dash
6	large orange twist	to garnish

EQUIPMENT Muddler, bar spoon

METHOD Muddle the orange slice in a tumbler and discard, but leave the juice. Half-fill the glass with cubed ice and the cherries, then pour over the remaining ingredients (except for the garnish) as well as the muddled orange slice. Stir with a long bar spoon for about 30 seconds. Top up with more ice and stir. Twist the orange skin over the drink to release its oils, dropping it into the glass afterwards.

GLASS TYPE:
TUMBLER

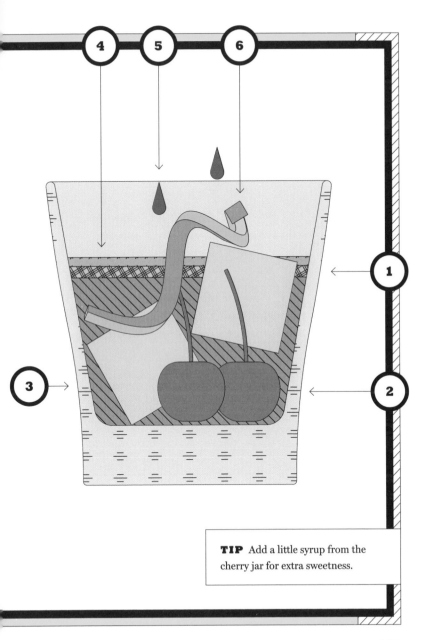

TIP Add a little syrup from the cherry jar for extra sweetness.

THE NEW CLASSICS

CLASSIC TEQUILA COCKTAILS, REWORKED FOR MODERN TIMES. WE'VE WAGGLED REPOSADO AT A MOJITO AND SUPER-CHARGED AN ESPRESSO MARTINI. LIKE ALL THE BEST THINGS IN LIFE, ALL YOU NEED IS A LITTLE TWIST.

TEQUILA SOUR

A modern twist on the Sour, this powerful cocktail has a delicate foam, smooth texture and zesty aroma. The dash of bitters adds a delightful aromatic edge. Imagine a smaller, punchier Margarita. As with all egg-white cocktails, serve super chilled.

INGREDIENTS

1	mezcal	60 ml (2 oz)
2	lime juice, freshly squeezed	30 ml (1 oz)
3	Simple Syrup (page 38)	15 ml (½ oz)
4	egg white	15 ml (½ oz)
5	Angostura bitters	dash
6	lime zest	to garnish

EQUIPMENT Shaker, strainer

METHOD Fill a shaker with ice, add all of the ingredients (except the bitters and garnish) and shake vigorously until the shaker is frosted. Strain into a glass. Add a dash of bitters and top with the fresh lime zest.

GLASS TYPE:
HIGHBALL

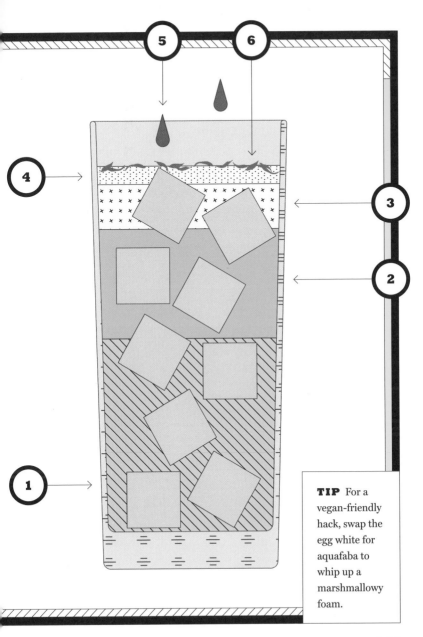

TIP For a vegan-friendly hack, swap the egg white for aquafaba to whip up a marshmallowy foam.

MEXICAN MOJITO

The classic Cuban cocktail masterpiece with a Mexican twist. The white rum is replaced with a spike of reposado to give it a darker, more Caipirinha-like edge. Get messy with the muddler, bashing the flesh out of the ripe lime and unlocking the aromatic flavours of the mint leaves.

INGREDIENTS

1	lime	1
2	fresh mint leaves	8–12
3	reposado tequila	37½ ml (1¼ oz)
4	Demerara Simple Syrup (page 38)	15 ml (½ oz)
5	soda water	to top up
6	fresh mint sprig	to garnish

EQUIPMENT Muddler, bar spoon

METHOD Cut the lime into quarters and muddle with the mint leaves in the bottom of a glass. Add the tequila, syrup and half-fill with ice. Churn with a bar spoon to mix everything together thoroughly. Top up with soda water and more crushed ice, and churn once gently. Garnish with a small sprig of mint.

GLASS TYPE:
COLLINS

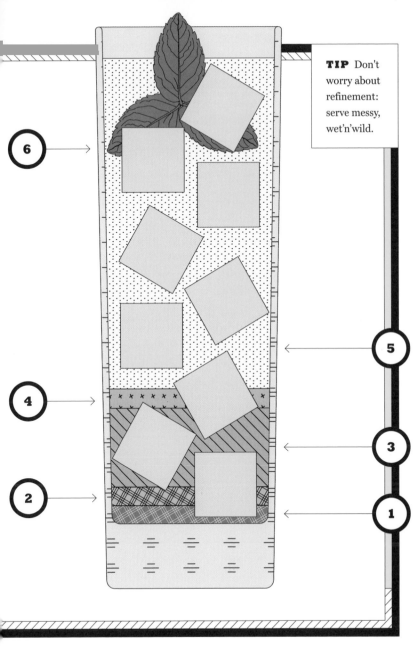

TIP Don't worry about refinement: serve messy, wet'n'wild.

ESPRESSO MARTINI

The legendary cocktail that's rocket-fuelled countless hen nights, the early hours of wedding parties, and pepped up sleep-deprived new parents at five-year-old birthday shindigs. It works perfectly with tequila, which spikes through the sweetness to keep you wide-eyed for hours.

INGREDIENTS

1	silver tequila	60 ml (2 oz)
2	Coffee Tequila (page 35 or you can use Patrón)	15 ml (½ oz)
3	Demerara Simple Syrup (page 38)	15 ml (½ oz)
4	cooled espresso	shot
5	coffee bean	to garnish

EQUIPMENT Shaker, strainer

METHOD Pour all of the ingredients (except for the garnish) into a shaker filled with ice. Shake vigorously until the tin is frosty, then strain into a chilled glass. Float a coffee bean on the foamy top.

GLASS TYPE:
MARTINI

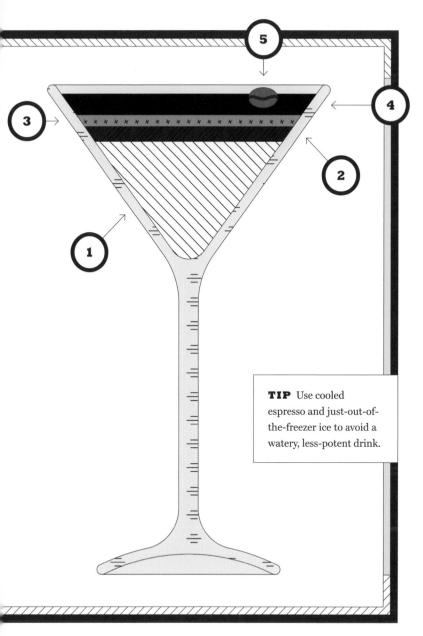

TIP Use cooled espresso and just-out-of-the-freezer ice to avoid a watery, less-potent drink.

MARACUYA SOUR

Passion fruit is the zesty power house behind this delicious mezcal sour. The flavour combination is sweet and tart, and the mezcal creates a smoky, singed edge. Make it long by swapping out the egg white or aquafaba and serving in an ice-filled highball topped with chilled soda.

INGREDIENTS

1	mezcal	60 ml (2 oz)
2	passion fruit purée	60 ml (2 oz)
3	Simple Syrup (page 38)	15 ml (½ oz)
4	lime juice, freshly squeezed	15 ml (½ oz)
5	egg white or aquafaba	1
6	fresh mint leaves	4–5
7	passion fruit half	to garnish

EQUIPMENT Shaker, strainer

METHOD Pour all of the ingredients (except the garnish) into an ice-filled shaker. Shake vigorously until frosty and foamy, then strain into a chilled glass. Garnish with half a passion fruit.

GLASS TYPE:
COUPE

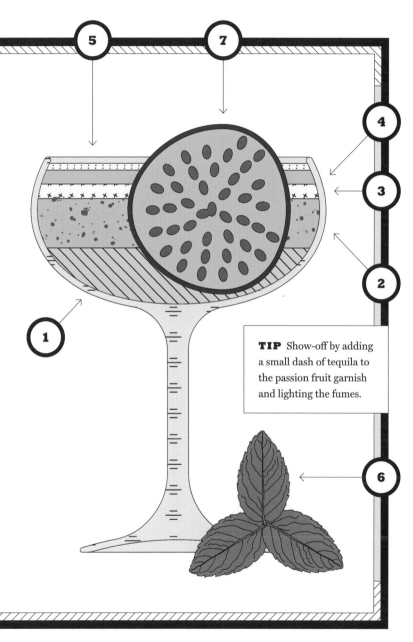

TIP Show-off by adding a small dash of tequila to the passion fruit garnish and lighting the fumes.

THE MARGARITAS

A SHARP, SOUR SLAP OF LIME, THE SWEETNESS OF ORANGE LIQUEUR, THE TANG OF SALT AND THE PEPPERY POWER-PUNCH OF TEQUILA: THE MARGARITA WAS CREATED IN THE 1940S BY US BARTENDERS (THE EXACT CREATION STORY IS MIRED IN MYTH) IN A BID TO CREATE THE WORLD'S FRESHEST, ZINGIEST, MOST POWERFUL, MOUTH-CAVING TEQUILA COCKTAIL. THEY NAILED IT.

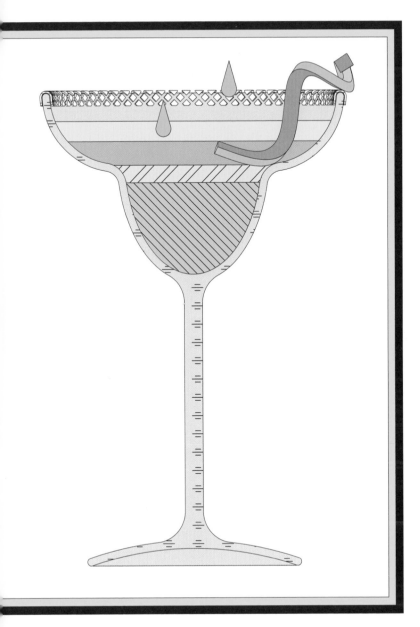

THE PERFECT MARGARITA

If it ain't broke... Perfectly balanced, this classic cocktail must be sipped ice cold and, once your eyes uncross, you can make another.

INGREDIENTS

1	lime wedge	for salt rim
2	sea salt	for salt rim
3	silver tequila	60 ml (2 oz)
4	triple sec	30 ml (1 oz)
5	lime juice, freshly squeezed	30 ml (1 oz)
6	lime twist	to garnish

EQUIPMENT Shaker, strainer, saucer for the rim

METHOD Squish a lime wedge along the edge of a chilled glass and dip in sea salt. Shake the tequila, triple sec and lime juice vigorously over ice and strain into the glass. Garnish with the lime twist.

GLASS TYPE:
MARGARITA OR
LARGE WINE

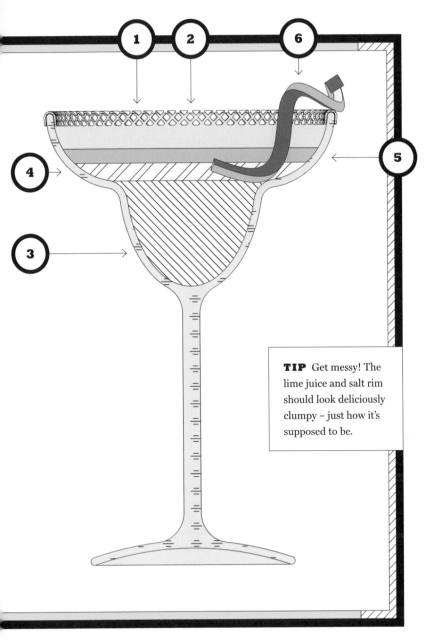

TIP Get messy! The lime juice and salt rim should look deliciously clumpy – just how it's supposed to be.

BREAKFAST MARGARITA

Struggling to balance your love of toasted sliced sourdough and zingy citrus preserve with living your best gluten-free life? Swap out the bread for tequila. This Margie kick-starts boozy brunches and post-night out recovery sessions. Worth setting your alarm clock for.

INGREDIENTS

1	reposado tequila	45 ml (1½ oz)
2	orange liqueur	22½ ml (¾ oz)
3	lime juice, freshly squeezed	22½ ml (¾ oz)
4	orange marmalade	1 heaped tsp
5	Simple Syrup (page 38)	7½ ml (¼ oz)
6	orange twist	to garnish

EQUIPMENT Shaker, strainer

METHOD Add all of the ingredients (except the garnish) to an ice-filled shaker and shake until cold. Strain into an ice-filled glass and add an orange twist.

GLASS TYPE:
TUMBLER OR JAM JAR

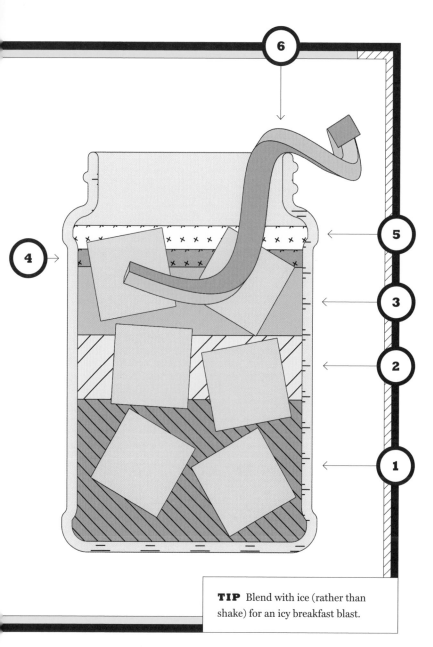

TIP Blend with ice (rather than shake) for an icy breakfast blast.

PINK GRAPEFRUIT AND CHILLI MARGARITA

The delicate pink blush of this unbelievably fresh-tasting Margarita belies a subtle chilli heat that will leave your lips tingling.

INGREDIENTS

1	lime wedge	for salt rim
2	sea salt	for salt rim
3	gold tequila (or use Chilli Tequila, page 36)	60 ml (2 oz)
4	orange liqueur	15 ml (½ oz)
5	pink grapefruit juice, freshly squeezed	30 ml (1 oz)
6	lime juice, freshly squeezed	30 ml (1 oz)
7	agave syrup	15 ml (½ oz)
8	thin fresh jalapeño slices	3 slices
9	fresh jalapeño slice	to garnish

EQUIPMENT Shaker, strainer, saucer for salt rim

METHOD Squish a lime wedge along the edge of a chilled glass and dip in sea salt. Add all of the ingredients (except the garnish) to a shaker filled with ice. Shake vigorously and strain into the glass. Garnish with a slice of jalapeño.

GLASS TYPE:
MARGARITA OR
LARGE WINE

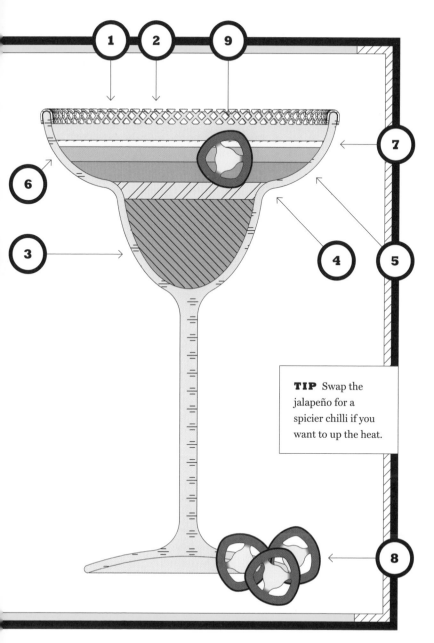

TIP Swap the jalapeño for a spicier chilli if you want to up the heat.

FROZEN BLOOD ORANGE MARGARITA

This dark pink, slushie-style drink is *muy* delicious, and blending until smooth makes this the easiest, speediest way to mainline a Margie – plus, the juice is one of your five-a-day.

INGREDIENTS

1	lime wedge	for salt rim
2	sea salt	for salt rim
3	silver tequila	45 ml (1½ oz)
4	triple sec	15 ml (½ oz)
5	blood orange juice, freshly squeezed	60 ml (2 oz)
6	agave syrup	15 ml (½ oz)
7	lime juice	dash

EQUIPMENT Blender, saucer for salt rim

METHOD Squish a lime wedge along the edge of a chilled glass and dip in sea salt. Add all the ingredients (except the lime juice) into a blender with a scoop of crushed ice. Blend on high speed until mixed. Pour into your glass and top with a dash of lime juice.

GLASS TYPE:
MARGARITA OR
LARGE WINE

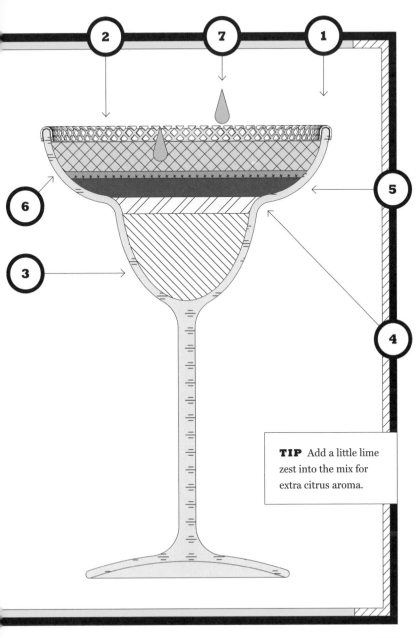

TIP Add a little lime zest into the mix for extra citrus aroma.

GOLDEN SHOWER

Smooth gold tequila and a dash of fresh orange dials up the classic pale lime-coloured cocktail to a bright, golden yellow tone. Slightly less tart than your usual Margarita, it also works as a delicious pitcher cocktail – perfect if you've invited some friends over for a golden shower party.

INGREDIENTS

1	lime wedge	for salt rim
2	sea salt	for salt rim
3	gold tequila	45 ml (1½ oz)
4	orange liqueur	15 ml (½ oz)
5	lime juice, freshly squeezed	30 ml (1 oz)
6	lemon juice, freshly squeezed	30 ml (1 oz)
7	orange juice	dash
8	orange twist	to garnish

EQUIPMENT Shaker, strainer, saucer for salt rim

METHOD Squish a lime wedge along the edge of a chilled glass and dip in sea salt. Place all of the ingredients (except the garnish) into a shaker over ice, shake vigorously and then strain into the glass. Garnish with an orange twist.

GLASS TYPE:
MARGARITA OR
LARGE WINE

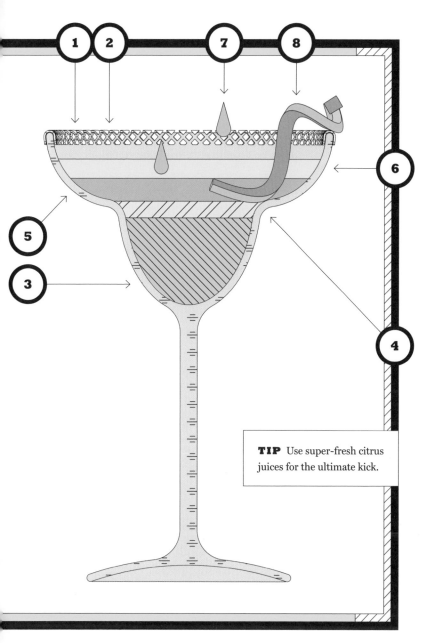

TIP Use super-fresh citrus juices for the ultimate kick.

FROZEN MANGO MARGIE

Your mangoes need to be perfectly ripe, squishy and aromatic for this recipe to be at its best. Mango and tequila are perfect bedfellows, and the pinch of sea salt intensifies the flavour.

INGREDIENTS

1	silver tequila	30 ml (1 oz)
2	fresh mango, peeled	½
3	lime juice, freshly squeezed	30 ml (1 oz)
4	triple sec	15 ml (½ oz)
5	agave syrup	15 ml (½ oz)
6	sea salt	pinch
7	chilli flakes	pinch
8	lime wedge	to garnish

EQUIPMENT Blender

METHOD Place all of the ingredients (except the chilli flakes and garnish) into a blender with a scoop of crushed ice and blend until smooth. Pour into a glass and very lightly sprinkle with chilli flakes. Garnish with a lime wedge.

GLASS TYPE:
MARGARITA OR
LARGE WINE

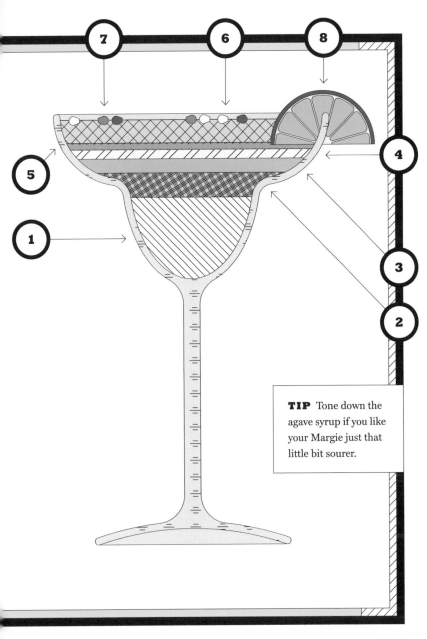

TIP Tone down the agave syrup if you like your Margie just that little bit sourer.

THE LARGERITA

Great things are created when two delicious things are merged into one. The Largerita has a classic Margie base, but it's topped with a smooth, sparkling beer. Perfect for backyard BBQs.

INGREDIENTS

1	mezcal	60 ml (2 oz)
2	orange liqueur	27½ ml (¾ oz)
3	lime juice, freshly squeezed	30 ml (1 oz)
4	Mexican beer	120 ml (4 oz)
5	lime wheel	to garnish

EQUIPMENT Shaker, strainer

METHOD Add the mezcal, orange liqueur and lime juice to a shaker filled with ice. Shake vigorously until the tin is frosty, strain into a chilled glass and top up with beer. Garnish with a lime wheel.

GLASS TYPE:
HIGHBALL

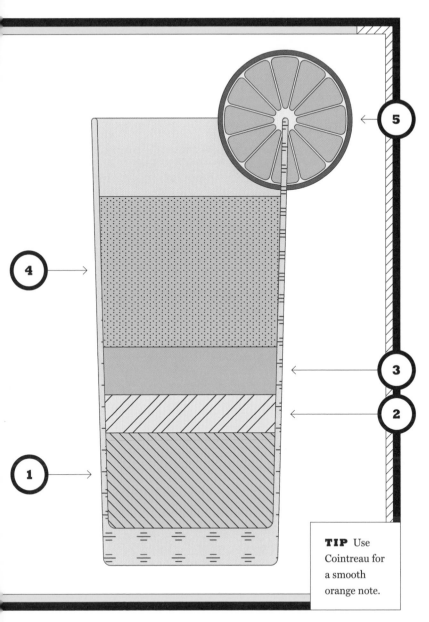

TIP Use Cointreau for a smooth orange note.

THE
FRUITY
ONES

TEQUILA'S ORIGINAL BEDFELLOW IS CITRUS
JUICE – THE FRESH SQUEEZING OF LIME, LEMON
AND GRAPEFRUIT – AND THEIR PUNGENT PEEL
– ELEVATE THE SPIRIT TO AN
OTHERWORLDLY LEVEL.

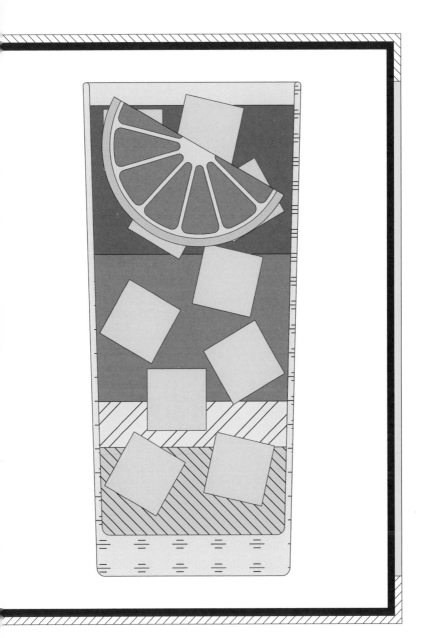

TEQUILA SPRITZ

This muddled, fruity soda-topped spritz is summer in a glass (without the heat rash and mosquito bites). Smooth gold tequila, a bright zingy citrus mix, and squash-ripe strawberries. A perfect balance between sweetness and a heady sourness, with refreshing soda water.

INGREDIENTS

1	large strawberries	4
2	Simple Syrup (page 38)	15 ml (½ oz)
3	gold tequila	45 ml (1½ oz)
4	lime juice, freshly squeezed	½
5	lemon juice, freshly squeezed	½
6	orange juice, freshly squeezed	1
7	soda water	to top up
8	strawberry	to garnish

EQUIPMENT Muddler, bar spoon

METHOD Muddle the strawberries in a glass with the syrup. Fill the glass three-quarters of the way with crushed ice and pour over the tequila and juices. Mix together with a bar spoon and top up with soda water. Garnish with a strawberry.

GLASS TYPE:
HIGHBALL

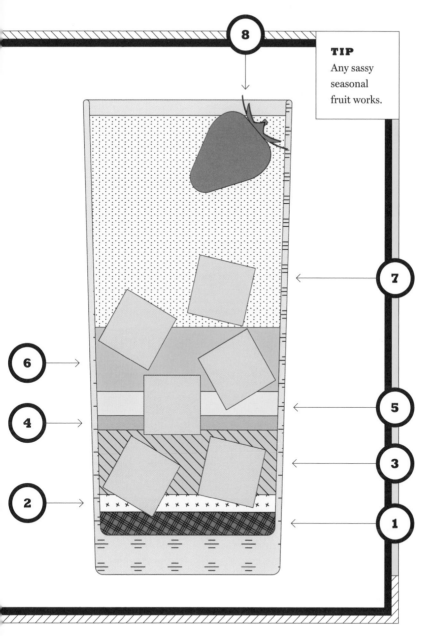

TIP
Any sassy seasonal fruit works.

ICED WATERMELON FIZZ

Imagine a chilled watermelon blended into an icy-fresh, slushie-style cocktail that's packed with booze. The Iced Watermelon Fizz is a blended cocktail topped up with tonic water for extra sharpness. Serve with tequila-laced watermelon slices, because why not?

INGREDIENTS

1	silver tequila	45 ml (1½ oz)
2	lime juice, freshly squeezed	15 ml (½ oz)
3	triple sec	15 ml (½ oz)
4	agave syrup	15 ml (½ oz)
5	peeled watermelon chunks	handful
6	tonic water	to top up
7	watermelon slice	to garnish

EQUIPMENT Blender

METHOD Blend the ingredients (except the tonic and garnish) with a small scoop of crushed ice until slushy. Pour into a glass and top up with tonic. Garnish with a slice of watermelon.

GLASS TYPE:
HIGHBALL

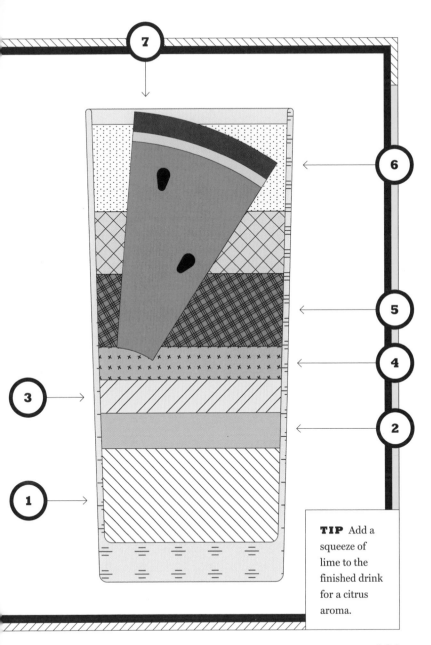

TIP Add a squeeze of lime to the finished drink for a citrus aroma.

SUNBURN

This ruby-toned cocktail has a dry, rather grown-up edge, powered by cranberry and blood orange juice and smoothed out with buttery gold tequila. This works perfectly as a solo drink.

INGREDIENTS

1	gold tequila	37½ ml (1¼ oz)
2	orange liqueur	15 ml (½ oz)
3	blood orange juice, freshly squeezed	60 ml (2 oz)
4	cranberry juice	60 ml (2 oz)
5	blood orange slices	to garnish

EQUIPMENT Bar spoon

METHOD Pour all of the ingredients (except the garnish) into a glass filled with ice. Stir well and add the blood orange slices to garnish.

GLASS TYPE:
HIGHBALL

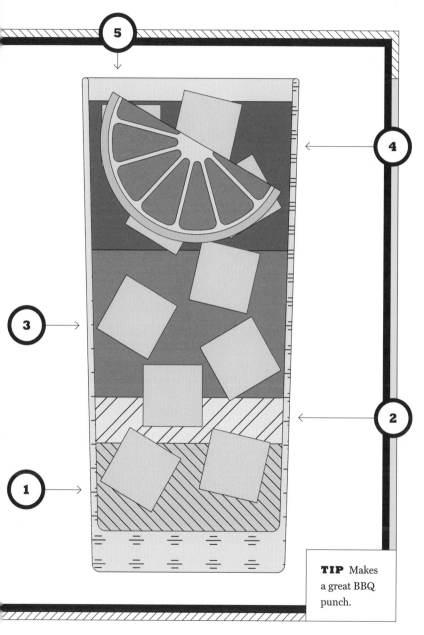

TIKI TEQUILA

Tiki culture, a product of 1940s and 1950s US cocktail scenesters, and (very) loosely inspired by Polynesian carvings, is a much-beloved booze art form. This recipe is a wink to the original tiki cocktail, the Mai Tai, with fresh silver tequila and aromatic orange blossom. Add as many tacky garnishes as you can.

INGREDIENTS

1	silver tequila	45 ml (1½ oz)
2	orange curaçao	15 ml (½ oz)
3	apricot liqueur	15 ml (½ oz)
4	pineapple juice, freshly juiced	60 ml (2 oz)
5	lime juice, freshly squeezed	15 ml (½ oz)
6	orange blossom water	dash
7	grenadine	dash
8	pineapple wedge and leaf	to garnish

EQUIPMENT Shaker, strainer

METHOD Pour all of the ingredients (except the garnish) into an ice-filled shaker, shake vigorously and then strain into an ice-filled glass. Garnish with a pineapple wedge and leaf.

GLASS TYPE:
TIKI GLASS

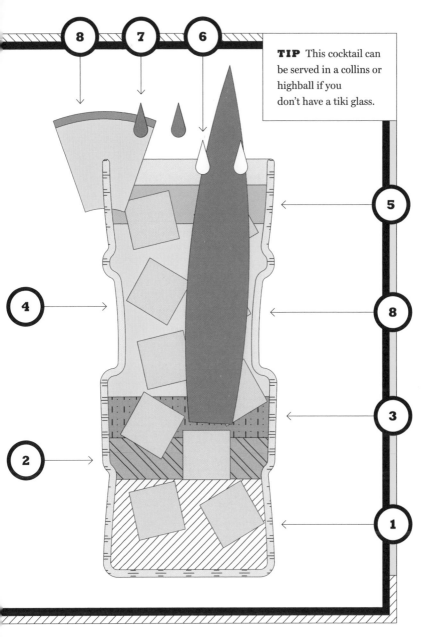

TIP This cocktail can be served in a collins or highball if you don't have a tiki glass.

SPEED RUNNER

This two-tone cocktail is impossibly fruity and complex with fresh strawberries, a banana aroma, and buttery smooth gold tequila with a rum float on top. Partial to a Daiquiri or Colada-style drink? This is your new best friend.

INGREDIENTS

1	gold tequila	45 ml (1½ oz)
2	strawberries	60 g (2 oz)
3	banana liqueur	22½ ml (¾ oz)
4	crème de mûre	22½ ml (¾ oz)
5	lime juice, freshly squeezed	15 ml (½ oz)
6	dark rum	15 ml (½ oz)
7	strawberry slices	to garnish

EQUIPMENT Blender

METHOD Add the tequila, strawberries, banana liqueur, crème de mûre and lime juice to a blender with a scoop of crushed ice. Blend until well mixed. Pour into a glass and carefully float the dark rum on top. Garnish with fresh strawberry slices.

GLASS TYPE:
LARGE WINE GLASS

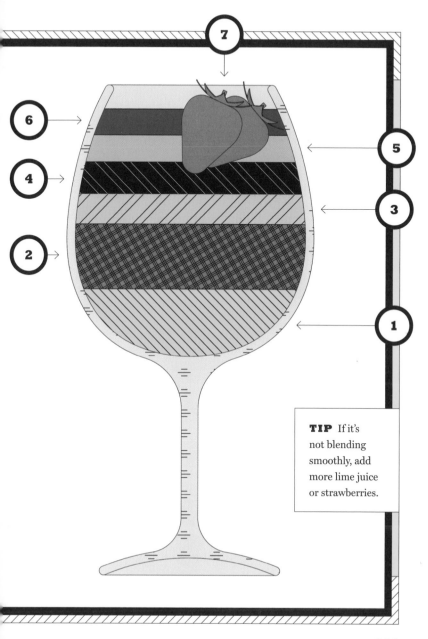

TIP If it's not blending smoothly, add more lime juice or strawberries.

PIÑA TEQUILA

The classic coconut cocktail, spiked with silver tequila and an embarrassing amount of cocktail umbrellas, plastic monkeys and curly straws.

INGREDIENTS

1	silver tequila	37½ ml (1¼ oz)
2	coconut rum	15 ml (½ oz)
3	pineapple juice, freshly juiced	60 ml (2 oz)
4	orange juice, freshly squeezed	30 ml (1 oz)
5	lime juice, freshly squeezed	15 ml (½ oz)
6	pineapple slice	to garnish

EQUIPMENT Shaker, strainer

METHOD Add all of the ingredients (except the garnish) to a shaker filled with ice and shake vigorously until cold. Strain into an ice-filled glass. Garnish with the pineapple slice.

GLASS TYPE:
HIGHBALL

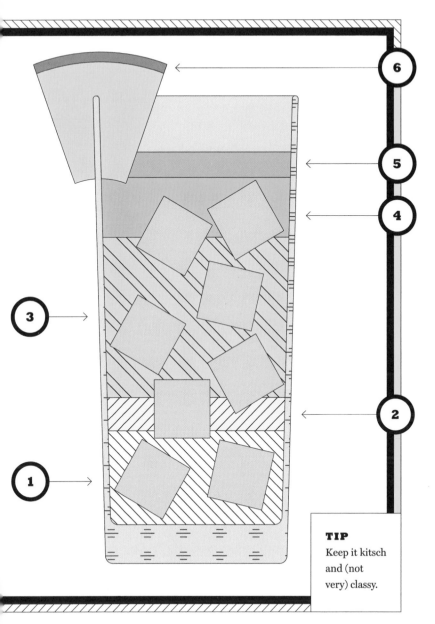

TIP
Keep it kitsch
and (not
very) classy.

MINTBERRY TULEP

A minty, muddled blueberry-powered tequila cocktail that lifts the spirits (and is packed full of them, too). Super fresh with a fruity profile and underpinned by silky smooth gold tequila.

INGREDIENTS

1	fresh mint leaves	6
2	blueberries	6
3	gold tequila	60 ml (2 oz)
4	lime juice, freshly squeezed	30 ml (1 oz)
5	Demerara Simple Syrup (page 38)	dash
6	sprig of mint	to garnish

EQUIPMENT Muddler, shaker, strainer

METHOD Muddle the mint and blueberries together in a shaker, then add the remaining ingredients (except the garnish). Fill with ice cubes and shake vigorously. Strain into a julep cup filled with crushed ice and garnish with the sprig of mint leaves.

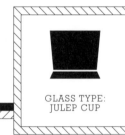

GLASS TYPE:
JULEP CUP

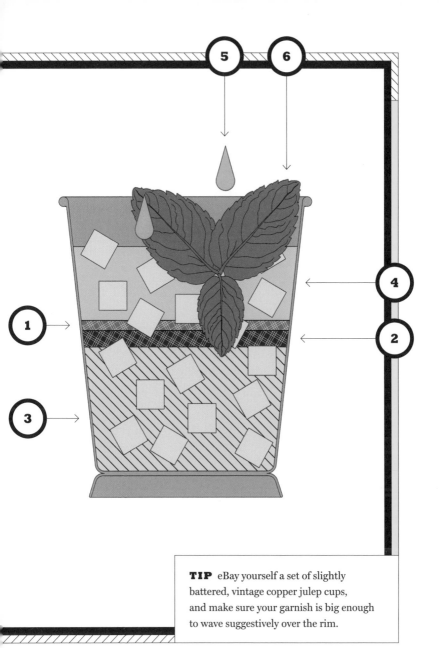

TIP eBay yourself a set of slightly battered, vintage copper julep cups, and make sure your garnish is big enough to wave suggestively over the rim.

CEREZADE

Frangipane and jam, in a glass. Smooth gold tequila, ruby-toned cherry juice, ripe citrus and a little almond liqueur. Top up with a tart lemonade to keep things sweet, or swap with chilled soda water for a little extra freshness.

INGREDIENTS

1	orange wedge	1
2	lemon wedge	1
3	mezcal	45 ml (1½ oz)
4	cherry juice	30 ml (1 oz)
5	Simple Syrup (page 38)	15 ml (½ oz)
6	almond liqueur	15 ml (½ oz)
7	Angostura bitters	dash
8	clear lemonade	to top up

EQUIPMENT Muddler, shaker, strainer and bar spoon

METHOD Muddle the orange and lemon wedges in a shaker and fill with ice. Add the mezcal, cherry juice, syrup, almond liqueur and a dash of bitters. Shake hard to chill. Strain into a glass filled with ice and top up with clear lemonade. Churn once gently with a bar spoon.

GLASS TYPE:
HIGHBALL OR COLLINS

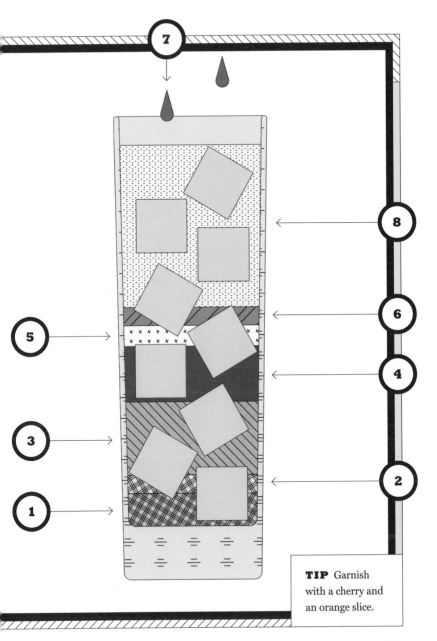

TIP Garnish with a cherry and an orange slice.

THE
SPICY
ONES

IS IT GETTING HOT IN HERE?
MEXICO'S PREMIER SPIRIT GOES PERFECTLY
WITH A LITTLE SPICE. HERE'S TO CHILLI,
JALAPEÑO AND FIERY GINGER TEQUILA
COCKTAILS TO HEAT THINGS UP.

GINGER SNAP

Tequila and ginger are the perfect won't-come-downstairs-until-the afternoon bedfellows. The 'Snap' is the perfect celebration of both flavours, with a spicy jalapeño kick. It's sweet, spicy, sour and aromatic – all in one hit. Swap tequila for mezcal for a deeper, gruffer taste.

INGREDIENTS

1	lemon	½
2	preserved ginger	1 slice
3	jalapeño	2 thin slices
4	gold tequila	45 ml (1½ oz)
5	agave syrup	7½ ml (¼ oz)
6	Angostura bitters	dash
7	ginger beer	90 ml (3 oz)
8	lemon wedge	to garnish

EQUIPMENT Muddler, bar spoon

METHOD Cut the lemon half into wedges and muddle together with the ginger and jalapeño slices in a glass. Add the tequila, agave syrup and bitters and half-fill with crushed ice. Stir gently to mix everything together. Top up with ginger beer. Add more ice and do a single churn with the bar spoon. Squeeze a lemon wedge over to garnish.

GLASS TYPE:
HIGHBALL

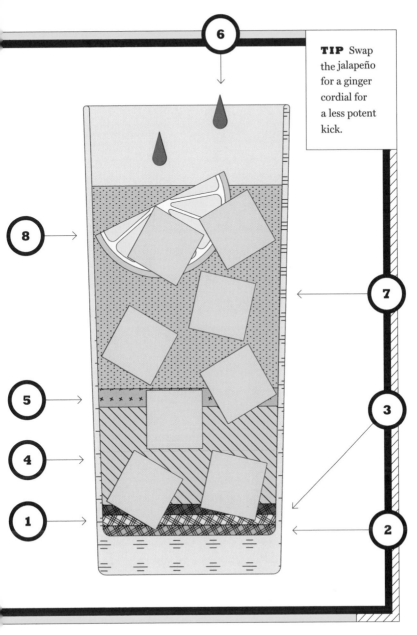

6

TIP Swap the jalapeño for a ginger cordial for a less potent kick.

PERKY PEAR

This fruity, gingery dessert of a drink is an autumnal favourite: excellent as a single drink and perfect for a punch, too. It works with off-the-shelf pear nectar, but it's best with juicy chunks of ripe pear flesh, skinned and blended with ice. Make sure your pears are extremely perky.

INGREDIENTS

1	silver tequila	45 ml (1½ oz)
2	ripe pear chunks, peeled	handful
3	lime juice, freshly squeezed	15 ml (½ oz)
4	cardamom bitters	dashes
5	ginger beer	to top up
6	lime wedge	to garnish
7	pear slice	to garnish

EQUIPMENT Blender, strainer

METHOD Pour the tequila, a handful of ripe pear chunks, the lime juice and bitters into a blender with 3–4 cubes of ice. Strain into a glass filled with ice and top up with the ginger beer. Squeeze a wedge of lime over the drink and drop a pear slice into the glass.

GLASS TYPE:
HIGHBALL

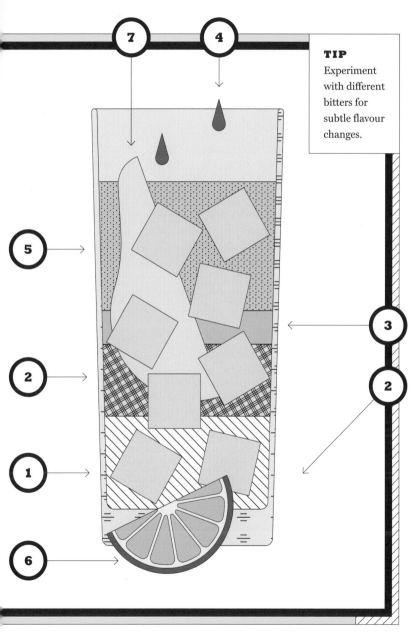

TIP
Experiment with different bitters for subtle flavour changes.

THE DIABLO

Feeling horny? The Diablo will sort that out. It's one of the most iconic tequila recipes and there's a reason why: it's deliciously moreish and has a subtly spicy kick. Muddled ripe lime, buttery gold tequila, a little crème de mûre and fiery ginger ale. Serve with crushed ice, lime wedges and salacious

INGREDIENTS

1	lime	¾
2	gold tequila	37½ ml (1¼ oz)
3	crème de mûre	15 ml (½ oz)
4	fiery ginger ale	120 ml (4 oz)
5	lime wedge	to garnish

EQUIPMENT Muddler, bar spoon

METHOD Cut the lime into wedges and muddle in a julep cup or jam jar, then fill three-quarters of the way. Pour in the tequila and crème de mûre, stir to mix and top up with ginger ale. Top up with more crushed ice and a wedge of lime.

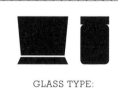

GLASS TYPE:
JALEP CUP OR JAM JAR

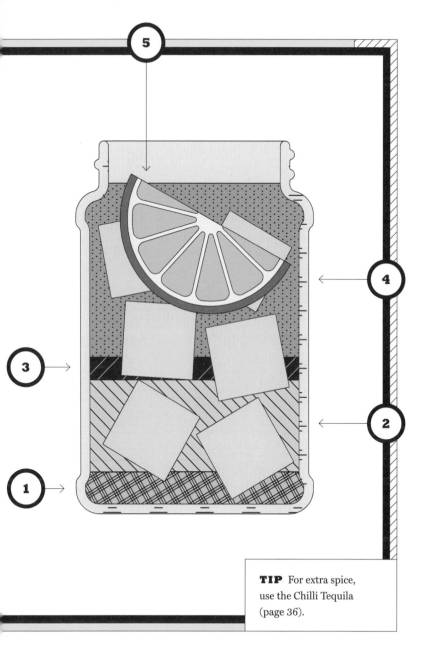

TIP For extra spice, use the Chilli Tequila (page 36).

POMEGRANATE COSMO

The traditional Cosmopolitan gets a bad rap: its feverish popularity in the 1990s makes it almost retro today. This reposado and pomegranate cocktail is a contemporary version, without losing any of its charm. Serve super chilled.

INGREDIENTS

1	lime wedges	3
2	reposado tequila	37½ ml (1¼ oz)
3	orange liqueur	15 ml (½ oz)
4	cranberry juice	30 ml (1 oz)
5	pomegranate juice	30 ml (1 oz)
6	pomegranate seeds	to garnish

EQUIPMENT Muddle, shaker, strainer

METHOD Muddle the lime wedges in a shaker, fill with blended ice and add the rest of the ingredients (except the garnish). Shake vigorously, then strain into a chilled glass. Sprinkle over the pomegranate seeds to garnish.

GLASS TYPE:
MARTINI

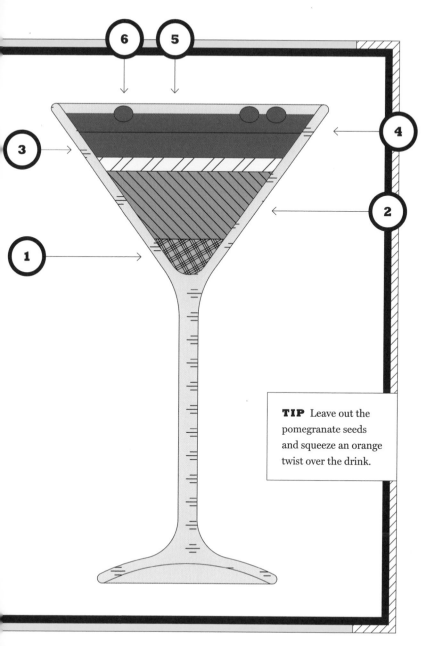

TIP Leave out the pomegranate seeds and squeeze an orange twist over the drink.

AGAVE ICED TEA

Imagine the most delicious cup of tea you've ever tasted. Now, imagine it with tequila, lime and agave syrup. Mind-blowing, right? This twisted iced tea recipe uses gold tequila, gold rum and ginger ale with a little agave sweetness.

INGREDIENTS

1	gold tequila	15 ml (½ oz)
2	vodka	15 ml (½ oz)
3	gold rum	15 ml (½ oz)
4	triple sec	15 ml (½ oz)
5	lime juice, freshly squeezed	15 ml (½ oz)
6	agave syrup	15 ml (½ oz)
7	ginger ale	to top up
8	lime wedge	to garnish

EQUIPMENT Shaker, strainer

METHOD Pour the tequila, vodka, rum, triple sec and lime juice into a shaker with ice and shake until frothy and cold. Strain into an ice-filled glass. Top up with ginger ale and garnish with a lime wedge squeezed on top.

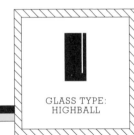

GLASS TYPE:
HIGHBALL

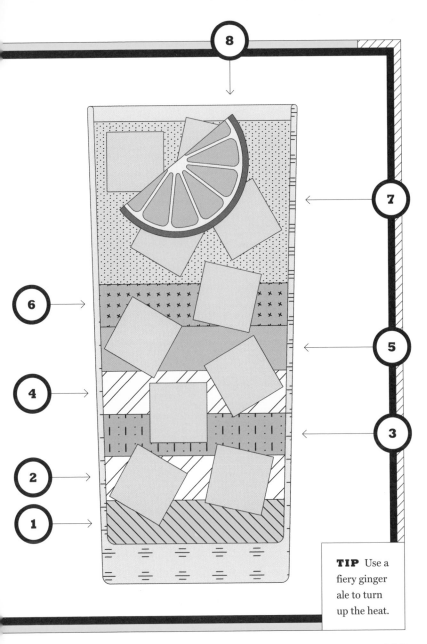

TIP Use a fiery ginger ale to turn up the heat.

THE

SHOOTERS

PREMIUM TEQUILA MIGHT BE STRICTLY
FOR SIPPING, BUT SOMETIMES IT'S BEST
TO THROW CAUTION TO THE WIND AND GET
IT DOWN YOU AS QUICKLY AS POSSIBLE.
PRESENTING, THE SHOOTERS.

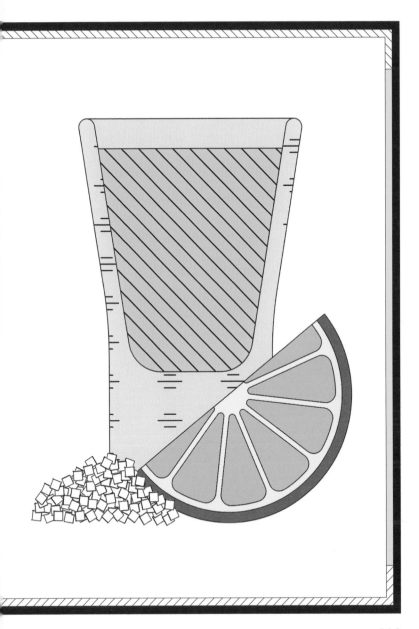

HEAD LIKE A HOLE

This precocious little shooter is surprisingly delicious, but with a lethal spiciness that will leave your lips tingling. It's sweet, strong and almost uncomfortably spicy – but you'll never have just one. Watch out, it'll put hair on your chest.

INGREDIENTS

1	white sambuca	15 ml (½ oz)
2	mezcal, straight from the freezer	15 ml (½ oz)
3	hot sauce	3 drops

METHOD Pour the sambuca into a shot glass, then carefully pour in the cold tequila so that it sits on top of the sambuca in a separate layer. Add 3 drops of hot sauce. Drink in one shot.

GLASS TYPE:
SHOT

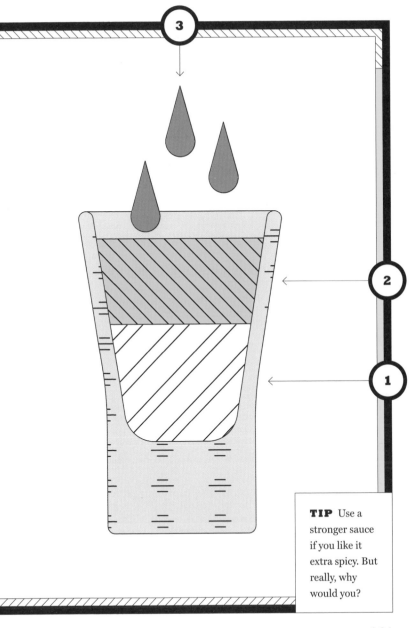

TIP Use a stronger sauce if you like it extra spicy. But really, why would you?

LICK DRINK BITE

One of the most prolific ways to drink tequila, yet the one that most people seem to get back to front. Lick the salt, drink the tequila, bite the fruit. Freeze the tequila first for an icy, less powerful-tasting shot.

INGREDIENTS

1	gold tequila	30 ml (1 oz)
2	sea salt	large pinch
3	lime or blood orange wedge	1 per shot

METHOD Pour a shot of tequila into a shot glass. Put a little sea salt on the back of your hand. First, lick the salt, then shoot the tequila. Finally, suck the lime.

GLASS TYPE:
SHOT

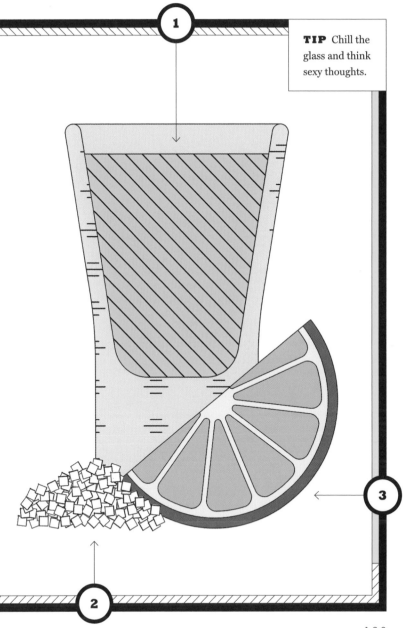

TIP Chill the glass and think sexy thoughts.

1

2

3

SANGRITA CHASER

Traditionally sipped alongside tequila, there are hundreds of Sangrita recipes, all with a tomato juice and grenadine base. This spicy version can be made ahead of time and kept in the fridge: perfect for shots and Bloody Marias.

INGREDIENTS

1	tomato juice	450 ml (16 oz)
2	Clamato juice	450 ml (16 oz)
3	lime, freshly juiced	½
4	orange, freshly juiced	½
5	Tabasco	dash
6	Worcestershire sauce	dash
7	grenadine	dash
8	soy sauce	dash
9	horseradish	½ tsp
10	green chilli, minced	1
11	salt and pepper	to season

EQUIPMENT Kilner bottle

METHOD Mix all of the ingredients together, bottle and leave in the fridge for at least 24 hours. Serve chilled in a shot glass alongside a good sipping tequila.

GLASS TYPE:
SHOT

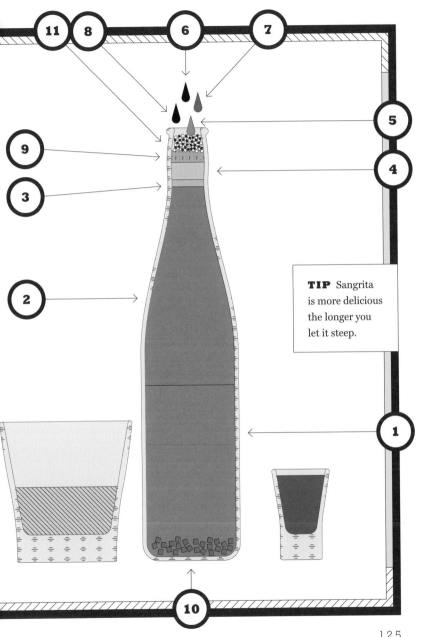

TIP Sangrita is more delicious the longer you let it steep.

THE BOILERMAKER

There are two ways to drink the Boilermaker: one is chilled and refined, the other dramatic and messy and over in seconds. Both are delicious. Serve each element super chilled.

INGREDIENTS

1	lime wedge	for salt rim
2	Flavoured Salt (page 39)	2–3 tsp, for salt rim
3	Sangrita Chaser (page 124)	30 ml (1 oz)
4	beer (Mexican or any sort)	330 ml (12 oz) bottle
5	mezcal	37½ ml (1¼ oz)

EQUIPMENT Shaker, strainer, saucer for the rim

METHOD Squish a lime wedge along the edge of a frozen glass and dip the glass in the salt. Pour the Sangrita Chaser into the frozen glass. Top up with very cold beer until the glass is two-thirds full, then fill a shot glass with mezcal. Either drop the shot glass into the beer and down the lot, or drink responsibly and sip both drinks with your pinky finger sticking out.

GLASS TYPES:
HIGHBALL AND
SHOT

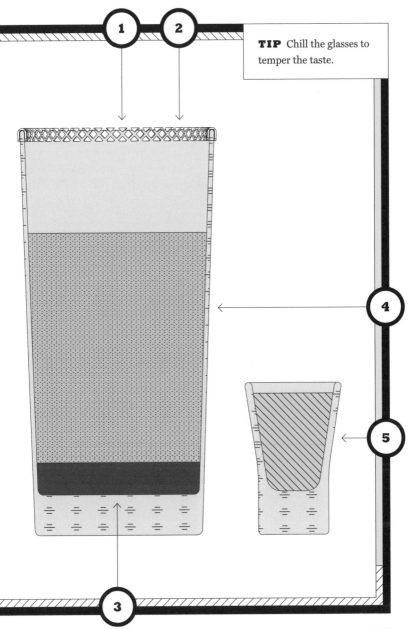

TIP Chill the glasses to temper the taste.

THE PUNCHES

THERE'S SOMETHING BRILLIANTLY RETRO ABOUT THE COMMUNAL DRINK, FROM SPIKED HIGH SCHOOL PROM PUNCHES IN 80S TEEN FLICKS TO THE BIG-BATCH PITCHER COCKTAILS OF 90S-THEMED BARS. HERE ARE SOME OF THE BEST.

BACKYARD SANGRIA

A delicious twist on the classic Sangria recipe, with smooth gold tequila, floral elderflower, wine and a ridiculous amount of citrus slices and berries.

INGREDIENTS

1	gold tequila	60 ml (2 oz)
2	orange juice, freshly squeezed	30 ml (1 oz)
3	pineapple juice, freshly juiced	30 ml (1 oz)
4	elderflower cordial	30 ml (1 oz)
5	agave syrup (or Simple Syrup, page 38)	30 ml (1 oz)
6	red, white or rosé wine	1 bottle
7	blood orange slices	to garnish
8	lemon slices	to garnish
9	seasonal berries	to garnish

EQUIPMENT Jug, bar spoon

METHOD Fill a jug with ice and pour in all of the ingredients, including the citrus fruit and berry garnish. Stir thoroughly.

GLASS TYPE:
PUNCH GLASSES OR
TUMBLERS

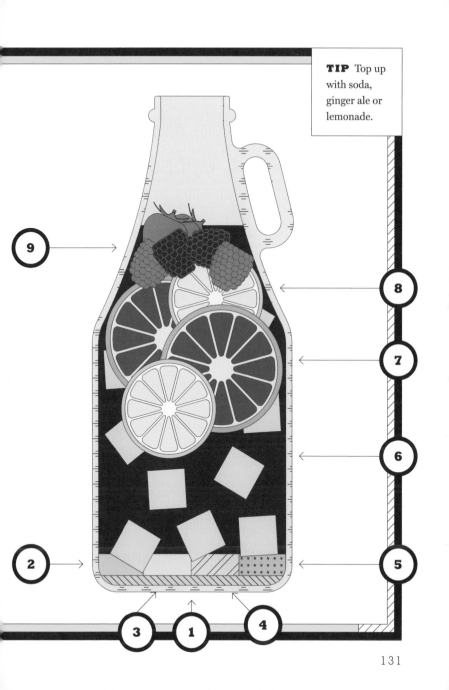

TANGERINE DREAMS

A glut of tangerines bashed into submission, afloat in a lagoon of tequila, Aperol and chilled soda. Delicious, aromatic and moreish. This Aperol Spritz-like punch is the perfect summer party addition.

INGREDIENTS

1	Aperol	200 ml (7 oz)
2	reposado tequila	200 ml (7 oz)
3	tangerines, freshly juiced	7
4	soda water	300 ml (10½ oz)
5	tangerine wedges	to garnish

EQUIPMENT Jug, bar spoon

METHOD Add the Aperol, tequila and tangerine juice to a large jug filled with ice. Stir the mixture before topping up with soda water and adding the tangerine wedges. Churn gently to combine.

GLASS TYPE:
PUNCH GLASSES OR
TUMBLERS

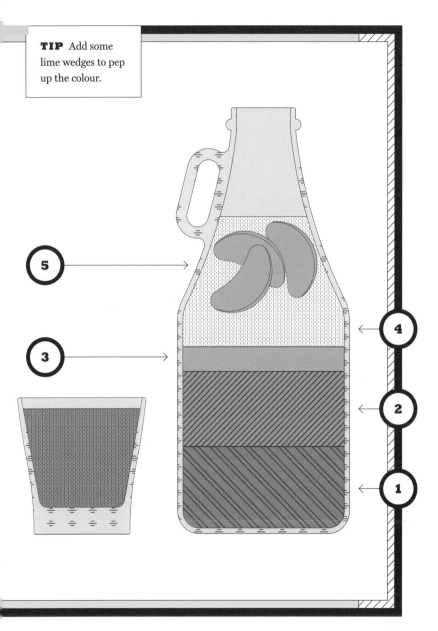

TIP Add some lime wedges to pep up the colour.

HOT AND STEAMY

IT'S NOT ALL ABOUT MUDDLING BERRIES AND
SQUISHING LIMES: TEQUILA IS THE PERFECT
SPIRIT TO SPIKE HOT DRINKS, FROM
A TURNED-UP TODDY TO A HOT CHOCOLATE
THAT'LL BLOW YOUR SOCKS OFF.

TEQUILA TODDY

A hot, hot, hot spin on the classic toddy, swapping out whisky for cinnamon-infused tequila and sweetened with honey and agave. If this marvellous medicine doesn't cure the winter sniffles, at least it'll numb the senses.

INGREDIENTS

1	Cinnamon Tequila (page 36)	60 ml (2 oz)
2	honey	7½ g (¼ oz)
3	agave syrup	7½ ml (¼ oz)
4	lemon juice, freshly squeezed	22½ ml (¾ oz)
5	cinnamon stick	1
6	cloves	2
7	hot water	120 ml (4 oz)
8	dried orange wheel	to garnish

METHOD Place all of the ingredients (except the garnish) in a mug or glass. Give it a good stir, then leave to steep for a few minutes before serving with a dried orange wheel.

GLASS TYPE:
HEATPROOF GLASS
OR MUG

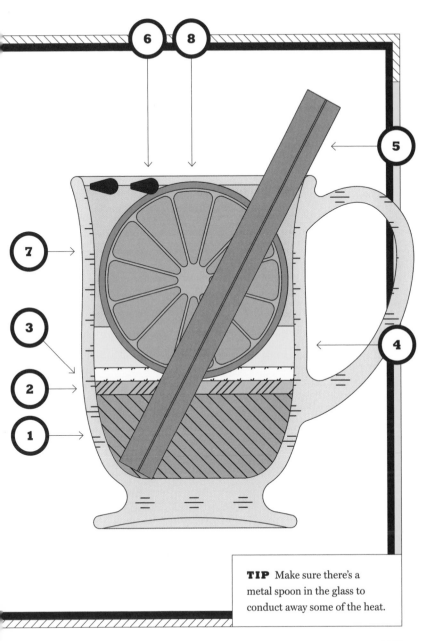

TIP Make sure there's a metal spoon in the glass to conduct away some of the heat.

MEXICAN HOT CHOCOLATE

This spiked hot chocolate is sweet and rich with a subtle chilli heat and eye-crossingly intoxicating aroma. Cardamom is, of course, not particularly Mexican, but it's a delicious addition.

INGREDIENTS

1	milk	200-250 ml (7-9 oz)
2	dark chocolate	3 squares
3	cocoa powder	1 tbsp
4	brown sugar	1 tsp
5	cardamom pod, bashed open	1
6	cayenne powder	pinch
7	mezcal (or Chilli Tequila, page 39, if you want a kick)	60 ml (2 oz)
8	whipped cream	to garnish
9	grated chocolate	to garnish

EQUIPMENT Saucepan

METHOD Warm the milk in a saucepan and add the chocolate, cocoa powder, sugar, cardamom pod and cayenne. Heat gently until all the ingredients have combined. Pour the mezcal into a mug and add the warm chocolate mixture. Top with whipped cream and grated chocolate (and a little extra cayenne, if you wish).

GLASS TYPE: MUG

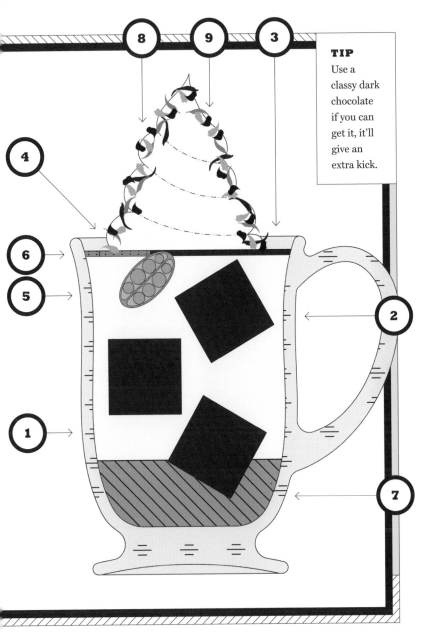

INDEX

ABOUT
DAN JONES

Perhaps the world's most prolific cocktail enjoyer and author of *GIN: Shake, Muddle, Stir* and *Rum: Shake, Muddle, Stir*, Dan Jones is a writer and editor living in London. A self-professed homebody, he is well versed in the art of at-home drinking and loves to entertain, constantly researching his cocktail craft and trying out new recipes.